Wait until Tuesday

John M. Garrett

Copyright © 2017 John M. Garrett.

All rights reserved. No part of this book may be used or reproduced by any means, graphic, electronic, or mechanical, including photocopying, recording, taping or by any information storage retrieval system without the written permission of the author except in the case of brief quotations embodied in critical articles and reviews.

LifeRich Publishing is a registered trademark of The Reader's Digest Association, Inc.

LifeRich Publishing books may be ordered through booksellers or by contacting:

LifeRich Publishing
1663 Liberty Drive
Bloomington, IN 47403
www.liferichpublishing.com
1 (888) 238-8637

Because of the dynamic nature of the Internet, any web addresses or links contained in this book may have changed since publication and may no longer be valid. The views expressed in this work are solely those of the author and do not necessarily reflect the views of the publisher, and the publisher hereby disclaims any responsibility for them.

Any people depicted in stock imagery provided by Thinkstock are models, and such images are being used for illustrative purposes only.
Certain stock imagery © Thinkstock.

ISBN: 978-1-4897-1108-3 (sc)
ISBN: 978-1-4897-1109-0 (hc)
ISBN: 978-1-4897-1107-6 (e)

Library of Congress Control Number: 2016921096

Print information available on the last page.

LifeRich Publishing rev. date: 2/17/2017

♡ Introduction

<u>Wait Until Tuesday</u> is the story of the miracle of organ transplantation. It follows the life, the fears, the loves, the trials and the seven-month hospital wait of a heart transplant patient.

The book brings the reader details regarding the critical shortage of organs for transplant, and reasons for the shortage. The shortage of organs causes the death of approximately 1/3 of all recipients waiting on heart and liver transplant lists in the United States.

It has been estimated that at least 25,000 additional people could be saved annually if additional citizens consented to be donors.

The book is dedicated to the brave men, women and children who are friends or family of organ donors or recipients. Their courage, faith and support make the miracle of transplantation possible.

Organ donation represents the ultimate "gift of life". I have spoken with hundreds of friends and strangers regarding the process of becoming an organ donor. The American people look upon organ and tissue transplants favorably. Most studies indicate over 80% of adults are in favor of transplants, yet only 2% of those who die become organ donors due to fears, health factors, age and unknowns.

Special recognition should also be given to my immediate family; my wife Barbara, son David, daughter Beth, brother Joe and my parents Joseph and Mary Garrett of Arnold, Maryland. Many times during the extended hospitalization, it would have been easy to give up. They never gave up, and always gave me reasons to live.

My family and friends also offered much encouragement, and allowed me to include them as subjects in the book. I have always felt an individual is molded through their association with the many people they meet and experiences during their lifetimes.

I have been blessed with wonderful parents and brother, aunts and uncles and cousins. My wife Barb as well as Beth and David have supported me for almost a lifetime. My friends, many of whom you will meet in the book, offered endless encouragement before, during, and after the operation.

Most of all, I thank our God for everything...my family and friends...

the donor and his family...the health care professionals...and the support and faith He gave me during the process.

I hope <u>Wait Until Tuesday</u> will provide enjoyment to the reader, and encourage additional consideration for the readers to become potential organ donors. It is meant to be informative, to dispel taboos and misinformation about transplants, and to save lives.

If only one life can be favorably impacted by writing this book, the months of research and the hundreds of hours spent in compiling the information will have been worth the effort.

I have had the opportunity of leading an extraordinary life. The early years in a small community in a tiny town, reared when times were simple, seemed like an unusual beginning.

♡ Life on Spriggs Pond

Our family moved to the small town of Arnold, Maryland in the Spring of 1954. I was in the final months of the sixth grade.

Our little community, named Magothy Manor, was located on the Magothy River, a tributary of the Chesapeake Bay. We lived on Spriggs Pond, a small pond with an inlet leading to the river. The pond afforded some protection from the full force of the hurricanes that ravaged the river several times each year. The tide would rise, the gale force winds would bend the trees and tear out piers and snap ropes, and the errant boats would slam against the sea walls or float to shore. It was an exciting time in life...much less complicated than today's world.

My brother Joe was always ambitious, a trait that continues to serve him today. He was in the hard crab business back in the mid-fifties. The Chesapeake Bay and connecting rivers teemed with seafood, and pollution was not the big problem that we have today. We would set eel traps, catch the eels using dead crabs as bait, and deposit the eels into a salty brine which removed the slim.

The next morning, we would take the little row boat, with the four horsepower motor, and begin the long trip to the river, or in the event of a beautiful morning, to the entrance to the bay. The sun would begin to rise as the small motor groaned. The cool crisp saltwater splashed against the side of the boat as Joe threaded the trot line. The eels would be cut into slabs and fastened to safety pins on a trot line.

The trot line was a piece of rope about 400 to 600 feet long. About every six feet, we had placed a safety pin. We threaded the safety pin through the eel (the black part of the eel was the toughest part of the eel), and coiled the rope in a bushel basket. Each of the ends was connected to a plastic jug that clearly marked its location. The line, when taut, would stretch across the bottom of the river, and crabs would smell the bait, and begin to eat the eel. When the line was pulled in, the crabs would not notice that the line was being lifted from the bottom of the river to the surface.

Many times, they would notice only when Joe started to make the sweep with the long handled crab net. Joe was deadly with the net. Few crabs escaped his aim. He quickly deposited each crab in a bushel basket, as they were flailing and snapping at having been snatched from the safety of the river. We waited until the line had been completed, and sorted the catch..large crabs, females, soft crabs, peelers (crabs about to molt) and finally those that we threw back...too small. The Summers were kind to us...a simple existence.

♡ First Heart Trouble

In 1979, I was working at Aladdin Industries in Nashville, Tennessee as Manager of Division Accounting and Financial Analysis.

Aladdin was a privately owned company, with the majority stockholder being a gentleman named Victor Johnson. Aladdin was a global manufacturing concern with operations in Europe, and joint ventures in South America and Asia. It was one of the largest manufacturers of school lunch boxes, stainless steel and glass thermos products and kerosene space heaters in the world.

My position entailed working closely with the Vice-President of Operations and his staff, and interpreting financial results and predicting financial results based upon alternative courses of action. We had a close relationship with each other, as well as his staff of professionals. His name was Ken Jorgensen.

Ken was a progressive executive, and in the course of our relationship, we would learn a lot from each other. Ken's major forte was his ability to utilize the strengths of each of his managers. His top lieutenant was a man named Bill Cooper, who was probably the best manager that I've ever worked with.

Ken would organize retreats at a state park near Nashville, and invite his managers. We would spend several days discussing new ideas, problems or concepts. Each of the disciplines was well represented, including engineering, sales and marketing, materials management, and finance. One of the meetings took place near Christmas in 1979. It was during a retreat that the first hint of a problem occurred.

I was a heavy smoker at the time, and abused my body through a lack of exercise, excessive weight, heavy coffee drinking and improper sleeping habits. Although my father had experienced a triple bypass operation several years before, I was not alarmed...I was only 36 years old...only older people had heart problems.

After we arrived at the lodge, we were welcomed with large platters of cold cuts and alcoholic beverages, followed by a buffet with many types of meat and vegetables. I smoked, ate and drank to excess as the comraderie developed through the evening. Many of the guys wanted to play cards into the wee hours of the morning. I opted for a night's sleep. I had left my sleeping pills at home, and spent most of the night tossing and turning in bed.

The next few days were again filled with excessive eating and smoking, and I was somewhat relieved when the time came to return to Nashville. On the way back to the office, I remarked to a friend that we would be able to have a large plate of Southern fried chicken, a cafeteria specialty, if we hurried. The chicken was always a treat (Mr. Johnson's favorite food, I'm told), but was greasy. Sure enough, our arrival at the plant coincided with lunch. My friend and I ate a double portion of chicken, together with fried okra and pinto beans. After eating, I noticed a pressure in my chest, and quickly attributed the problem to overeating and a lack of sleep. I decided to have a relaxing afternoon answering and reading mail until I went home.

The chest pressure continued, and I again denied that I was having heart problems. I continued to light one cigarette after another. I finally called Tina Chilton, one of my secretaries, and asked if she could bring a cold rag into my office. When Tina appeared in the doorway, her face immediately expressed dire concern. She asked if I was o.k. as she dialed the company nurse. Within two minutes, the nurse appeared, and wanted to summon an ambulance. I became quite antagonistic when she suggested that I go to the hospital. I would not allow her to call, and felt that I was capable of driving the 28 miles home to our family doctor in Franklin. Finally, a compromise was reached...one of my cost accountants, a young man named Jeff Bigach, would drive me to Franklin in his car.

Jeff was obviously nervous as we began our trip. He became more anxious as the rear of the car began to shake and bump. He was having a flat tire as we were going around the expressway. He pulled to the side of the road and opened the trunk to pull out the tire jack and spare tire. He was having problems with the jack, and I reached into the trunk and yanked out the tire. Jeff became alarmed and told me to rest. I foolishly lit up another cigarette and leaned against the car until he had completed the change. We finally arrived at the hospital...Jeff was a nervous wreck. One of my major concerns was that I was not going to be able to smoke in the hospital. I was still attributing any problem to overeating.

I was in Williamson County Hospital for about a week, when my doctor ordered a stress test. He had also originally attributed my condition to an excess of eating and smoking, coupled with an inability of dealing with stress. When the stress test was complete, he suggested that I undergo a cardiac heart catheterization at St. Thomas Hospital in Nashville the day after Christmas. I was allowed to go home for Christmas, but was told to curtail all activities until the catheterization results were known.

Christmas was not eventful, as I began to worry about the heart cath. My Dad had a friend who once had died shortly after having a test, but I was also confident that I was too young to have serious heart problems. I entered St. Thomas Hospital on December 26, with the procedure scheduled for the next day.

The test results were not encouraging, as I had serious blockage in three of the arteries feeding the heart. The doctors recommended surgery on January 2, the earliest scheduled day for elective surgery. I asked if I could go home for a few days. The doctors said sure...If I wanted to risk death. I decided to spend the next few days, including New Year's Eve, in the hospital.

During the waiting period, the doctors told me about angioplasty, a new procedure which entailed the insertion of a small balloon within a catheter to the blocked arteries. The balloon would be inflated at the blockage, pressing and smoothing the plaque against the walls of the arteries, and allowing the blood to pass through the widened arteries. The procedure was new, and the advantages were numerous... I would be able to return to work in the following week instead of six weeks and the cost would be significantly less than a bypass operation. I opted for the new procedure since I was also assured that any complications would be treated immediately, and a bypass would be performed immediately if there were complications.

♡ First Operation

I still did not appreciate the seriousness of my illness. My thoughts were in returning to my position at Aladdin. The procedure did not go well. I was awake, and able to view the operation through a monitor above the operating table. I watched as the catheter snaked its way through the artery up to a blockage. When the balloon was inflated, I felt pain as I had never felt before. It was if someone had stuck a knife into my chest and twisted the blade. I yelled for the doctors to stop for a minute. Apparently, the blockage was more severe than anticipated, and the insertion into the opening had completely cut off the blood supply, with the plaque being much harder than anticipated. The balloon was not strong enough to compress the plaque. The doctors asked if I felt well enough for another attempt. I said yes, and the procedure was repeated with similar results. The pain was unbearable, and I asked the doctors to stop. One of them said that they were taking me next door to do the bypass operation.

♡ Out of Body Experience

I next remember an experience which confused me for many months. It was only after watching a talk show that I discussed the subject with Barb, since I was sure that I had imagined what had happened. It concerned an out-of-body experience.

I remember the sensation of being lifted from my body, very slowly, and being in a position where I was looking down at an operation. There were many people in the room, with countless gages and the sounds of surgeons and nurses quietly speaking to each other. I did not recognize any of the medical personnel, or the patient since everyone was clad, or covered, with medical gowns and masks. I remember being near the ceiling and rotating near the hot lights of the operating room.

I next experienced entering a tunnel. The tunnel was warm and dark, with a very bright light at the end of the tunnel. I had a sensation of tremendous speed, as I approached the bright light. The speed was greater than the fastest roller coaster, and I had a feeling of euphoria as I came nearer to the light.

When I came to the light, I was met by two silhouettes or shadows. The figures did not speak to each other, but seemed to communicate by thinking. One of the figures thought "Is he ready yet?". The other responded by thinking "No, he has two small children." The light was warm, there was a feeling of total euphoria and happiness. I think that I had temporarily entered the Kingdom of Heaven.

Almost immediately after the response of the second silhouette, I experienced a feeling of disappointment. I next remember waking up, hearing Barb speaking to me, and rubbing my hand. I felt cold. Waking up with the tubes, the monitors, and the pain was as close to Hell as I ever want to be.

♡ Recovery

The recovery went extremely quickly. I was walking in a few days, and immediately began to badger the doctors into letting me return to work. I was determined that I wanted to be better than I had ever been, to perform to higher standards than I had ever done before, and to out-think, and out-work everyone in the company. The doctor said that I had the worst "Type-A" personality of any of his patients.

♡ Previous Brushes With Death

In the 20 years prior to the heart trouble, I had several close brushes with death, including one during the teen years, and another as I was rising up the corporate ladder.

♡ Electrocution

During my senior year in high school, a friend had been electrocuted as he was sanding the side of a boat at his home. He was standing on a raft, holding an electric sander when a boat passed, creating a wave that washed across his feet. Death was immediate. Although the individual was not one of my best friends, we had played sports together. His death had a sobering effect on me.

Several days later, I wanted to prepare my small runabout boat for painting. It had rained the night before, but I had mowed our lawn and decided to sand the sides of the boat. I was sweaty, and decided to take a swim before working on the boat. On the way to the pier, I changed my mind again, deciding to grab the sander and work on the boat.

I leaned against the boat, and grabbed for the sander. When I touched the sander, the electricity grabbed my hand, and a surge of current went through my body. I fell against the ground, just missing tumbling into the lake. The sander would not drop, and the fight began to stay alive. I tried to scream, but the sound was muffled. I could not stand up. The back of my head began to bang against the soft, wet ground. I thought of my friend...is this what he was thinking during the last few moments of his life? How long would it take me to die?

I continued to fight with all of my strength. I was lucky to be in decent shape after a season of athletics. I continued to call out for help. Several people across the pond, about 200 yards away saw me, rushed to their phones, and called our home. Unfortunately, my Mom was in the basement, and did not hear the phone.

A neighbor was on his roof, fixing his television antenna, when he heard me yelling for help. He didn't know it was a person yelling for help, but rather suspected animals fighting on the pond. He dispatched several small children to the pond to determine the source of the commotion. The children sauntered to the fence, a distance of 100 yards, took a look at the teenager rolling on the ground, and walked back to the neighbor's house. The neighbor climbed down from the roof, walked down to the water's edge, jumped the chain-link fence, and rushed to my side. I tried to talk, to tell him not to touch the sander. He reached down, and grabbed the sander from my hand. I collapsed into the weeds.

I was taken to the family doctor, but had not experienced any damage other than superficial bumps and scratches. The moist ground, and weeds had been beaten down with an impression of a body clearly outlined.

I often wondered why I had not tumbled into the lake, and been electrocuted as my friend. As I waited for the many hours, and days, and weeks, and months for a transplant, I wondered why my life had been spared on that Spring afternoon in 1960.

♡ British Airways

I had been sent to Great Britain to review the accounting system of our company's subsidiary located in Hartlepool, close to the North Sea.

Overseas travel was always an adventure. In addition to the jet lag, one had to adjust to a change in climate, customs and food. Travel to England was probably as close as one can get to domestic travel, except for the tight security when catching a connecting flight. The security personnel were always courteous, even when checking for weapons or explosive devices.

I was always happy to be heading home after a week or more in England. On one particular trip, I was even more glad to see Nashville after a harrowing return flight aboard a British Airways 747 aircraft. The return trip had started off innocently enough.

I had boarded the aircraft, and was disappointed that I was unable to have an aisle seat. There were approximately 450 people aboard the aircraft as we taxied toward the runway for the trip to Washington. I had called my parents, who were going to pick me up in Washington. We were going to have a nice weekend together before I returned to Nashville.

Suddenly, the plane lurched and quickly dropped down. I remarked to the fellow sitting next to me that the British had the world's worst and bumpiest taxiways. The engines on the left side of the aircraft suddenly stopped, and the aircraft stopped moving.

A few seconds later, the pilot came on the intercom to announce the aircraft had struck a DC-9 on the adjacent crossover. The wing of our aircraft had hit the tail of the DC-9. The pilot matter-of-factorly mentioned we would be returning to the terminal for a visual inspection, to ascertain if our plane would be able to make the journey across the Atlantic. No one seemed to be concerned until one of the passengers on the other side of the aircraft made a crack about the wing falling off our plane. Everyone attempted to shift to the side of the damaged wing in order to assess the damage.

It was obvious that a visual inspection would not be required to determine if the plane was airworthy. My immediate concern was the 40,000 gallons of jet fuel in the wings and belly fuel tanks. One spark, and we would have been part of one of the worst aircraft catastrophes of all time. It was several years after the collision of the 747 aircraft on the runways of the Canary Islands, the worst civilian crash of all times.

The plane eventually made it to the terminal, where we waited 6 hours for a substitute aircraft. During the wait, the passengers were not allowed to call to the United States. I was worried that my brother, who was scheduled to pick me up at Washington, would hear of the damage and be concerned about my welfare. Finally, British Airways had the passengers scratch a message to be called to the states.

The news of the collision made the evening national newscasts. Our pastor at St. Andrew Lutheran Church, Eric Pearson, heard the news and called Barb to inquire if she had heard from me. Barb said no, that I was slated to land in Washington, instead of flying to Atlanta with a transfer to Nashville. It was only after I had landed in Washington that I had the opportunity of calling Barb to tell her, and only at that point did she realize that Pastor Pearson had seen the information on the news.

Before and after I waited for a transplant, I often wondered about the collision on the runway at London. If our plane had been moving faster, if the DC-9 had caused excessive sparking, if the wing of our aircraft would have spewed fuel on a hot engine, or if we would have been forced to evacuate the burning aircraft, the probability of survival was slim. I continued to wonder...why hadn't I died prior to the transplant?

♡ Letter From Jessica

Dear Mr. Garrett

I really enjoyed your presentation. It was interesting to me because my grandfather just had a heart attack this past December. I think it's amazing that you're still alive. You gave us great advise that we can still use. As my grandpa told me, "God must still have something planned for me". I think God still has something planned for you.

The person who wrote this letter,
Jessica

"He who has health, has hope; and he who has hope, has everything."
ARABIAN PROVERB

♡ Miracles Do Happen

My miracle began in 1980, when I underwent triple bypass surgery on January 2. I had experienced a large amount of chest discomfort in the previous month. The cardiologists recommended an experimental procedure which involved the insertion of a catheter into the arteries feeding the heart and the inflation of a tiny balloon within the catheter. The inflation of the balloon would, in turn, flatten the plaque build up and enable resumption of normal blood flow. Unfortunately, the procedure did not work, and I experienced a heart attack. I was taken to an adjoining room where the bypass operation was performed.

In 1987, I had a "minor" heart attack, which should have provided ample warning that more serious problems were ahead unless a complete change in lifestyle was implemented. I didn't revise my diet, exercise regimen or behavior modification.

♡ Heart Attack- October, 1987

The period between January, 1980 and October, 1987 was uneventful, health-wise. I had reverted back to an unhealthy lifestyle since the bypass surgery. I smoked heavily, did not exercise, and ate lots of foods that were not good for my arteries.

I had managed to secure a responsible and stressful job as a Product Line Controller with Cooper Power Systems. Cooper Industries was an excellent fast growth company, and demanded excellent results from its employees. I did my very best to satisfy, and balance, the requirements of local, division, and corporate personnel with reporting requirements.

I worked with an excellent staff, who performed their duties with a high degree of efficiency. I enjoyed going to work each morning, since each day represented a new and different challenge. I enjoyed being with a large group of caring professionals.

Each year, corporations require the development of an annual budget, consolidated to reflect forecast sales and earnings, for review by top management. Our budget presentation, held near the Pittsburgh airport, was composed of the operations of four manufacturing plants; Zanesville, Ohio; Nacogdoches, Texas: Lumberton, Mississippi and Matamoros, Mexico, a maquiladora operation.

The development of the budget, and analysis, is a mammoth job requiring a great deal of coordination and analysis, with many supporting schedules. I compared the compilation of the budget to childbirth. The Controllers of the individual plants produced much of the detail, and a young accountant in Zanesville, Mike Friel, would help in the consolidation.

In the weeks preceding the meeting, Mike and I spent many long and stressful hours attempting to make sense of the numbers, and complete the schedules. The operation in Mexico presented an additional challenge, since currency translations, as well as language differences made communication difficult.

The data was presented at the Division offices in Pittsburgh, and attended by my boss, Lyman Guidry, the General Manager, the Division Vice President of Finance, the Division President and various other Vice Presidents.

The agenda normally included an overview of the market conditions facing the company, and a review of projected sales. The overview normally lasted less than one hour. Attention would then focus on the myriad schedules and reporting package presented to each executive. Some of the sessions were quite spirited, as a clear understanding of all numbers was necessary. Although I was the chief spokesman during the process, there were occasions when I could not answer the micro-managed questions. I depended on Mike Friel to supply some of the answers. Mike usually had the answer. The meeting consumed close to eight hours.

As we headed for the car that evening, I felt every bit of energy had been pulled from my body. We were all relieved, since the day had produced a consensus regarding the direction of our company for the following 12 months.

The next morning, Saturday, I decided to work a few hours prior to attending David's soccer game. He and Barb would pick me up on the way to the field. I stopped at the local mall prior to going to work, and stopped for a hot cinnamon bun and a cup of coffee. As I sat in the car, I felt a sharp pain in my chest. I attributed the pain to the large meal of the night before, black coffee, the Marlboro cigarettes, and especially the heavy sugar icing on the bun. I felt I was experiencing a bad dose of indigestion. Several minutes later, the pain subsided. I drove to work.

After I had opened some mail, the pain returned. I was the only person in the office, and walked down the stairs to a canteen area and bought a Pepsi. I walked up the stairs to my office and drank the Pepsi. I foolishly smoked another cigarette, and the pain returned.

I continued to review the mail, and pondered a vacation day. I had averaged working over 70 hours per week during the previous six weeks, and thought that a rest was in order. The next few days would provide a needed relief. A few minutes later, the guard called to report the arrival of Barb and David.

I looked out the window. David was attired in his light blue soccer shirt, shin guards and white shorts. He was having a great season, averaging several goals per game. I locked the door and hurried down the steps.

The field was located several miles from the office, and as we traversed the hilly, winding road to the game, the discomfort returned. The pain was subsiding as we arrived at Maysville High School, site of the league. Barb knew something was wrong, due to the heavy sweating. I told her that I was feeling sick, but did not want to go to the hospital until the game was over.

We waited a few minutes, and walked across the practice field. Barb was noticeably upset, and wanted to go to the hospital.

The weather that afternoon was blustery. The concession stand needed an attendant, and I agreed to watch the operation, with a view of the field. I felt better being shielded from the elements, and there was a place to sit in the trailer. The game started, and I soon began to experience even greater discomfort on my chest. I sat down, but did not feel any relief. I asked one of the children to find Barb. Within a matter of seconds, she was by my side. The pain and sweat were becoming worse. She summoned a gentleman for help, who recommended an ambulance.

I wasn't sure if there was time for an ambulance to come, and told Barb to help me across the practice field to the car. We stumbled to the car. Barb opened the door, and I quickly reclined on the front seat. The pain subsided as we made the four mile journey to Good Samaritan Medical Center.

I had dodged a bullet. Despite all the warning signs, I had ignored the best advice.

Later testing showed the bypass surgery grafts were partly closed, the result of smoking, poor diet and a sedimentary lifestyle. Somehow, I had thought those things only happened to other people. I had foolishly believed the notion of invincibility.

♡ Start of A Long Journey

The day of October 5, 1988 was the start of a long journey. It began normal enough...and about mid-morning, I decided to test drive a car for my daughter Beth. We had canvassed many of the used car lots in Zanesville in the previous weeks, and had located a good candidate several days before.

I completed most of the work that had to be done for the week, and decided to stop for some Kentucky Fried Chicken prior to visiting the car lot. It was a beautiful autumn afternoon, although unseasonably warm. I ate the lunch in the car, and read the WALL STREET JOURNAL...this was to be the start of a relaxing weekend.

I picked up the car, and drove across town to our church, where Barb was doing some volunteer secretarial work. We had a bulk mailing to take to the post office, and I felt it was a good opportunity to try out the car. We delivered the mailing, and I drove her back to the church. I felt a little uncomfortable, but attributed the feeling to the heavy lunch and the warm weather.

Interstate 70 intersects Zanesville, and I decided to take the car on the highway, and to determine how it would handle under faster conditions.

I nudged the odometer gradually up to 65 miles per hour, and did not notice any shaking by the steering wheel, although the axis of the wheel was not horizontal...perhaps the car had been in an accident. I did notice a tightness in my chest, and beads of sweat forming on my forehead. I turned on the air conditioner, and waited for some relief...none came. I switched the air conditioner to its highest setting. Still no relief. I kept hoping that the pain would subside, but relief would not come.

I pulled the car into a Rax restaurant parking lot, hoping that perhaps a milk shake would ease the pain. I walked into the restaurant, ordered a vanilla shake, and walked back to the car. Still no relief. I started the car, switched the air conditioner on high, and debated whether to lay down on the front seat. Thinking that I might pass out, and not be able to signal for help, I decided against laying down. I decided to attempt to drive back to town on a back road. I knew that I was dying.

I maneuvered the car to the road, and said, "please God, don't let me die". I thought of Barb, Beth, and David. I knew that I would have to marshall all of my strength and facilities for the drive back to town. The comment to God was one of many that I would have prior to, and after, the transplant.

I made the trip to the church, climbed a flight of steps, looked into the secretary's office, and Barb was not in the office. There was a lady near the entrance way of the church waiting for a bag of groceries (a food pantry is housed at our church) and she asked if I was O.K. I shook my head and asked if she could find a blond-haired lady somewhere in the church.

She disappeared, and several moments later, I heard the voice of Anne England, a good friend who had also been volunteering that morning. I was laying on the floor in a fetal position...the pain was intense. Anne yelled for Barbara, and told the janitor to call the emergency squad...they were there in a matter of minutes. Barb came running, and knelt over me, and asked if I was O.K. I told her that I would be O.K. in a few minutes. We both knew that I was not doing well. I almost was wishing that I would die, the pain was so unbearable, but I felt that if I was able to arrive at the hospital, that I would be able to receive some pain killer.

The ambulance driver and medic put me into the ambulance, and attempted to start an IV. There was a long delay because they were unsuccessful in starting the IV. An argument ensued, with the driver refusing to proceed to the hospital until the IV was properly started. The medic stated that, in his opinion, I had not, or was not suffering from a heart attack. Anne England was screaming for them to start the ambulance, and take me to Good Samaritan Medical Center, located about 1 mile away. The ambulance pulled away from the church, turned on the siren, and headed toward the hospital.

When I arrived at the hospital, everything turned into a kaleidoscope of activity, as I attempted to become comfortable. Eventually, the pain subsided and I was admitted to the Cardiac Care unit.

The next morning, I commented to Barb that I wanted to be moved from the room in Coronary Care. She asked why I wanted to be moved, and I told her the man in the bed next to mine was in pain and moaned all night, and I was unable to get any rest. Barb said I was the only patient in the unit, and it was I who had moaned in pain all evening.

It was during the first evening that I met Brian Jones.

♡ Dr. Brian Jones

Dr. Brian Jones provided the initial care when I had the attack in October 1988. We met at Good Samaritan Medical Center when I was in the CCU. During my illness, Dr. Jones' skill and encouragement had the most profound effect upon me than any health care professional.

He performed several catherizations, and was the first person to recognize that a transplant was the only hope for survival. I didn't know what to think when he originally told me I needed a transplant, other than it was probably the most horrifying news that I had ever heard. I doubted that he was correct...it was the last time I would ever doubt him.

I found Brian Jones to be one of the most intelligent people I have ever met. His interests were so wide, and we could talk about anything. Even those subjects that I was versed in were easily understood by Dr. Jones. Barb bought me a book...WHY DO CLOCKS RUN CLOCKWISE? that pondered questions that I spent many minutes attempting to answer, and Dr. Jones answered spontaneously.

♡ Good Samaritan Medical Center

I spent three weeks at Good Samaritan Medical Center, during which time I was defibulated three times. I was "thumped" on numerous other times, when the nurses watching the heart monitor would notice irregularities on my heart beat...they would come running to the bedside, and hit me on the chest. Evidently, the knock on the chest was almost analogous to hitting a push button, as the heart would resume a normal rhythm.

♡ Emotions

Heart transplantation is an emotional roller coaster, with wide and turbulent mood swings. In order to have a successful experience, the patient must recognize that the swings will occur, and be able to deal with them.

When I was first told of the serious nature of the problem, I felt terrible fear, followed by denial, anger, acceptance, and finally, a desire to beat the problem. One of my hospital visitors was a Catholic priest, who had serious heart problems. He told me that when he found out that he required extensive surgery, he cursed God for giving him a bad heart, and the fact that he had never smoked or abused his heart, made the illness unbearable.

I told the priest that I was not mad at God, although I was perplexed because I had always attempted to be a good person, thinking that perhaps that being good would shield me from unpleasant things. I told the priest that I had been blessed during my lifetime with wonderful parents and a brother, as well as a wonderful wife and two very special children. I had managed to have many happy experiences, and perhaps my life would not be long, but rather short with many meaningful relationships. I was content at that point with my life, although I did regret that I had spent an inordinate amount of time pursuing a career, when we could have had more family activities.

♡ Samantha's Visit to the Hospital

When I was waiting at Good Samaritan Medical Center in Zanesville, to be transferred to Ohio State University for evaluation, I needed a morale booster. I asked Dr. Jones if I could go home for a few hours to see our animals. Of course, my condition precluded removal from the hospital.

Dr. Jones understood the importance of a patient's mental condition, and he consented to have Samantha brought to the hospital. Neither he, nor the staff, nor Barb told me that he had written the order to have Samantha brought to the room.

About 5 minutes before Samantha was brought up the back steps, one of the nurses told me that I was going to have a visitor. I noticed several groups of people near the room, but did not think that it was anything unusual.

Suddenly, I heard the click of toenails against the stone floor, and saw Barb following Samantha into the room. Samantha looked bewildered (she had a right to be bewildered), and surveyed the room and its contents. Her head turned quickly from side to side. I think my scent was masked by the other smells of the hospital. Suddenly I spoke, calling her name.

She stopped, turned her head and looked directly into my eyes. She started an uncontrollable whimper, and tried to jump into the bed. Alas, it was too high and she kept jumping and yelping. Barb helped her into the bed, and she continued to whine and wag her tail. What a great love affair! I looked around the unit. By this time, many of the nurses and support staff had come to the door, and I noticed many sniffles and handkerchiefs. It was a great thrill to have Samantha with me. Within several minutes, she was lying comfortably beside me, with her soft brown eyes never leaving me.

The visit was a great form of therapy. I later spoke about the incident with Barbara Mendelson, the Supervisor of the CCU section. She said that Samantha's visit was both the first, as well as the last, by an animal in the hospital's history.

During the stay at Good Samaritan, Dr. Jones stated that my heart had been severely damaged, and to consider the possibility of having a heart transplant. I suppose that there are more frightening things in the world than being told that you need a transplant…I just can not imagine what that would be. He suggested that I be transported to the Ohio State University Hospital for evaluation.

My friend George Steensen appeared several minutes after Dr. Jones told me the bad news. His presence comforted us.

♡ Lois and George Steensen

Lois and George Steensen attended St. John Lutheran Church in Zanesville. George was a retired Lutheran pastor, and later served as an interim pastor at St. John during the absence of a full-time pastor. Lois was active in the church, and for several years, we served together as members of the Church Council.

They were married late in life, and had one daughter, Kay, who had blessed them with a grandson, Bert, who brought George and Lois much happiness. George and Lois had a wonderful marriage. George often compared Lois with the Mona Lisa, who had the same type of smile.

George and Lois would visit me in the hospital, and provided us with encouragement during the first part of my illness. At one point, they became ill and were patients in the hospital. After some discussion, the administration at the hospital put them in the same room.

Lois's illness was diagnosed as cancer, and she put up a gallant fight before succumbing to the illness. I was a patient at Ohio State at the time of her death, and was unable to attend her funeral. I often think of Lois, her bravery and her suffering. I wonder how, and why, she endured all of the suffering. She was a wonderful lady.

I still see George. Sometimes, we go to lunch or dinner. His love for Lois still endures. He keeps busy trying to help others who are less fortunate. He loves to make wooden toys for children. His hobby was featured in the TIMES RECORDER, the local newspaper, and is a true labor of love.

♡ Transfer to Ohio State

The evaluation at Ohio State was delayed due to a large workload, and the critical task was to stay alive until I was transported to Ohio State in Columbus.

When I was being transferred, I was accidently spilled onto the asphalt at the emergency room when the wheels of the gurney rolled in a storm grate. I knew the future wasn't going to be easy. I was accompanied on the trip by Sandy Joseph.

♡ Sandy Joseph

Sandy Joseph was one of my favorite nurses. Sandy was always very efficient, and one Sunday, while watching the Cleveland Browns versus the Cincinnati Bengals, I felt myself slipping into unconsciousness. I said something to Sandy, and the next thing that I remember was looking up and seeing Sandy, together with several others, with the defibulator paddles. What a terrible sight! I mumbled that I was O.K. but the order was given to stand clear. I felt a hard, painful thump against my chest. Sandy's quick action had saved the day.

Sandy and I had another unforgettable experience when I was transferred to Ohio State University Hospital for the evaluation. We arrived at the emergency room entrance, and the gurney was removed from the ambulance. I was strapped down, and had several intravenous solutions being administered, as well as oxygen. The legs of the gurney were extended, and the cart began to roll toward the door. Sandy was holding the I.V. solutions, and the attendants were talking.

The wheels of the gurney fell into a storm grating. The world suddenly turned upside down, and the cart flipped over onto me. My arm suddenly was bloody and full of cinders, and Sandy was totally shocked. She quickly gained her composure and tried to clean up my face and arms. I later found out that Sandy, upon her return to Zanesville, asked to go home. Her concern for my health and well-being was representative of many nurses during my illness.

♡ Rod and Mindy Nelson

Our family met Mindy and Rod Nelson shortly after we had joined our church in Zanesville. Mindy and Rod were a young couple who recently adopted a wonderful, bright and articulate daughter named Molly. Mindy and Pat Mast were at Ohio State, during the evening that Jim and Cheryl Couts had driven a long distance through a snowstorm during a particularly harrowing period.

Rod and Mindy had met while they were attending Kansas State University. Rod's job as a radio and television announcer had brought them to Zanesville. Mindy was active in various church and gardening activities. My confinement in the hospital brought many letters and cards of encouragement from their family.

♡ Evaluation at Ohio State

The tests did not go well at Ohio State. In addition, my family was summoned to the hospital on several occasions due to numerous failures...I seemed to be getting worse. On one occasion, I was put on a balloon machine, where a slit was made in my groin, and a catheter was positioned in my heart. The balloon would expand and contract, in order to assist the heart with the pumping function. I later learned that the use of the machine was usually a last resort, due to severe complications sometimes encountered.

I was told that I was not a good candidate for a transplant because my blood tests indicated that I had Hepatitis. Several hours later, I was told that a mistake had been made in the lab, and it would not be a problem!

I was also told that because of my height, I was not a good candidate, because the donor would have to be about the same size. I was also told that because I was a blood type "**O**" there was a huge demand for the universal heart. I became extremely disheartened.

I became even more aware of the strain on my family. My Mom and Dad, as well as my brother drove to Columbus from Maryland to be at my side. I remember them entering the room, and my Dad looking at me, hugging me, and sitting in a chair by the window. It was almost completely dark, and I could hear him sobbing, and clearing his throat. What a sad time it must be for any parent to watch a son or daughter dying. The strain was as visible on my brother Joe, as well as my Mom.

♡ The Living Will

As the days wore on, the strain became greater, and I decided it was not fair to impose the mental torture on my family. I asked my Dad and Joe to draft a living will for my signature. I requested that should additional measures be required to keep me alive, I be allowed to have a dignified death, without other extreme medical mechanical devices, such as respirators or a Jarvik heart.

They drafted the will, had it witnessed, and presented it to the cardiologist. He promised to do his very best to allow me to return home with medication in order to relieve the pain. I honestly feel that he did not expect me to live more than a few days without benefit of mechanical devices.

My brother Joe suffered with me, as the pain continued.

♡ Joel Garrett

I have been blessed in my lifetime to have had a wonderful brother.

Joe was born about four years before me. We were close as youngsters. I recall an incident as we were growing up in Baltimore that will always be remembered, as it showed a brotherly love that has been sustained through our many years.

We were playing a game of softball in a vacant lot in northern Baltimore. Joe always selected me for his team, since I was the smallest kid on the block, and no one else wanted me on their team. One afternoon, I was running for a ball, slipped, and fell on a broken beer bottle hidden in the grass. The jagged edged immediately punctured deeply into my knee. The blood gushed through the pants, and I called to Joe for help. He rushed to my side, saw the blood, and immediately turned grey. He helped to take me home where Mom took us to the hospital. Joe was there during the emergency when I was a little boy, and the vigil continued when his brother faced death in a hospital room in Columbus, Ohio.

Joe drove to Columbus with Mom and Dad when the cardiologist felt my condition was extremely critical. At one time, there were countless IV solutions being administered, a Foley catheter had been inserted to carry some of the body wastes into a plastic bag at the edge of the bed, and a catheter had been inserted in my groin, attached to a balloon and residing at the heart to help it pump.

I was told not to move under any circumstances, since movement would cause the position of the balloon catheter to change, perhaps causing instant death. I was in the position for many days. I had severe pain in my left leg, and frequently pleaded for either a hot or a cold treatment to alleviate the discomfort. Joe began to massage my leg, as well as lifting and moving it in several positions.

Relief was immediate. Just as he had comforted me 40 years before, on a vacant lot in northern Baltimore, he was helping me to overcome pain during a period of extreme stress and discomfort.

♡ Confession to my Dad

Sometimes, strange things enter our minds as we are dying. Perhaps we are trying to cleanse our conscience, but one incident concerning my Dad came out during a particularly bleak time at Ohio State University Hospital.

I was in critical condition at the time. I had signed a living will to limit the amount of care given to me by the staff. I asked to talk with my Dad. He entered the room and took a position close to the bed. I began to tell him about the Studebaker Silver Hawk.

The incident with the Studebaker had occurred about 28 years before, but it would forever be a vivid part of my memory.

I had just received my driver's license, and had been driving the family car...a 1953 pink Studebaker (my Dad loved Studebakers, regardless of the color). As you might imagine, pink Studebakers were not "cool" with the other teenagers, and I was a little embarrassed when I drove it. My friends laughed at me. At least it was better than the 1950 Desoto that I sometimes drove.

In the Spring of 1960, Dad began to look for a sporty newer car, and located a 1959 Studebaker Silver Hawk. What a improvement from the pink car! He bought it from a used car dealer, and brought it home on a Friday evening. It was white, with a continental wheel on the trunk, red leather seats, and a large V-8 engine with a manual transmission...the car was built for speed.

I asked Dad if I could take the car out on the date that evening. He gave me the answer that I expected...NO! After much persuasion, Dad consented.

I picked up my date, and we proceeded to drive around Annapolis. I was hoping to see many of my friends, and to flaunt the new wheels to those friends who had laughed at the pink 1953 Studebaker. What a great life...a pretty date and a pretty car...this was living!

As the evening wore on, I became more familiar with both the new car and the date. Eventually, I put my arm around her shoulder, and we continued to cruise around town. Red lights began to cause problems, as I had to reposition my arm to shift gears. I wondered if the new car had a feature similar to the 1950 Desoto...could I shift gears without depressing the clutch?

Not only that, but I would shift with my left arm instead of the right arm. I attempted all these things at once, and heard several of the worst sounds that I had ever heard (or have heard up to now!). The transmission made a terrible grinding noise...really loud.

My stomach turned inside out...suddenly things weren't so great, because I didn't know how I would ever explain this calamity to Dad. I would rather walk home than tell Dad that I had maimed his new car. I was thankful that Dad would consider that Maryland had a death penalty before he killed me.

I managed to deliver my date to her doorstep, and to slowly nurse the car back home. I tried to develop a story to tell Dad, but nothing made sense. I decided to take the coward's way out, and tell him nothing. The next morning, Dad asked how the car had run.

I told Dad that the car had performed well, but the transmission had made some grinding noises on the way home. He immediately sprung up from the chair, and proceeded to charge out to the car. He was muttering that the used car dealer had sold him a car with a defective transmission...that story made sense to me! He turned the key, the engine started, and I prayed that somehow, the transmission had managed to repair itself...no such luck!

The awful sound was still there, as Dad attempted to pull out of the yard, onto the road. My heart sank...what if Dad asked me directly if I had ruined his transmission...could I manage to mount the courage to tell him the truth...and if I did, would my Brother let me live with him?

Fortunately, Dad never asked, but he did something that scared the daylights out of me...he jumped into the pink Studebaker, and we headed to the car dealer where he had bought the car. Dad was going to make the dealer repair the defective transmission!

We drove to the dealer, and Dad quickly located the salesman. He was quite vocal in his opinion that the dealer had attempted to sell him a car with a defective transmission. The salesman was adamant in arguing that the transmission was in perfect condition when the car was purchased.

I was petrified, since I knew exactly what had happened to the transmission. It was too late to confess, but beads of sweat were breaking out on my forehead, and the guilt pangs were almost overwhelming. The discussion became even more heated as the salesman called his supervisor into the fray. The boss defended the position of the dealership. This was awful...if there had been a hole deep enough to swallow me up, I would have gladly crawled into it.

Finally, an agreement was reached...the dealer would purchase the parts to fix the transmission (a nominal cost) but Dad would be responsible for the labor.

We returned home, and Dad proceeded to drive the car up on some blocks, crawled under the car and, after several minutes, disconnected the transmission. He carried the transmission into the basement, and placed it on his workbench. Within hours, the table was full of hundreds of pieces.

There were rings and clamps and screws and bolts and gears...I didn't know how anyone could possibly put all of the pieces back together. I, of course, kept wishing that I had not wrecked the transmission... and kept having guilty feelings.

Dad would analyze each piece. Finally, he found several pieces that had obviously been subject to cruel and unusual punishment. He quickly placed the parts in a bag, and we headed back to the dealer for the replacement parts.

When we arrived at the dealer, he quickly denied any guilt associated with the faulty transmission, and furnished the replacement parts. Dad and I returned home. The day had been exhausting for both of us, but for different reasons.

The next morning, Dad reassembled the transmission. As if by magic, each of the parts in the box and on the workbench disappeared into the transmission. Dad crawled back under the car, and within an hour, we were driving on the highway. The experience taught me several valuable lessons...never shift without pushing in the clutch, or always buy cars with automatic transmissions!

The rough times continued at Ohio State for over a week, as my condition worsened.

♡ Jim Couts

Jim Couts was a Lutheran pastor. Jim was somewhat of a free spirit, with a great sense of humor. We met in 1984 when his family and our family joined St. John Lutheran Church in Zanesville on the same Sunday. Jim was to serve as an Assistant Pastor.

He and his wife Cheryl had three children: Lori, Aaron and Andrew. He and Cheryl led a simple life, with Jim supplementing his church earnings with odd jobs, including a picture frame business. His goal in life was to start a tent ministry.

Jim was a dynamic speaker, and his sermons raised thought provoking questions. His eyeglasses did not always fit correctly, and were constantly slipping down on the bridge of his nose. His forehead contained deep furrows, and he often looked stern.

He was involved with the initial discussion for the development of Christ's Table, a warm meals program that fed over 54,000 meals in 1990 to the hungry in Zanesville.

Jim's loyalty and friendship were golden. During the darkest days of my illness at Ohio State, Jim was notified that I was in critical condition. He had been called to serve a church in Marietta, Ohio and technically was not our pastor. He and Cheryl drove 125 miles through a blinding snowstorm to be at my family's side in the middle of the night. His support will always be memorable.

Jim came to my room when I was on the balloon pump, a device that helps the heart to beat. Later that morning, he told some friends who had come to the hospital he was glad that they had made it to Columbus, because he was not sure that I could not make it through the night without a miracle. The miracle came.

Jim and his congregation were supportive during the illness. I had the opportunity of addressing some of the congregation in August when we visited his church. I told of the trials of being sick, and the miracle of God's work.

♡ Recovery and Return Home

Almost immediately after signing the living will, through the grace of God, I started to rally, and in a matter of days, was able to walk around the bed. Several days later, I walked around the CCU. Each day, I could feel God's hand helping me.

I came home on the day before Thanksgiving. What a wonderful day. A good friend of our family, Jan Tandy drove up to Columbus with Barb to bring me home. I watched the leaves as we drove home...the final vestige of Fall had turned most of the leaves to a dark brown, and most had collected on the ground. It was a cool afternoon as we pulled into the driveway. Several surprises were waiting, including flowers from friends and a bouquet of balloons from Barbara Mendelson. It was great to be home after six weeks in the hospital.

Our animals (Susie, our little black dog, and Samantha, our brown dog) gave me the greeting of a lifetime. They rolled on their backs and constantly yipped as they jockeyed for position, so as not to miss a single petting.

One of the wonderful things that God gives to us is the miracle of an animal's love. Animals do not demand much from us...only that we return a small portion of the loyalty and love that they give to us. I thought of one of our most beloved animals, a dog named Brandy.

♡ Brandy

All humans should have an animal friend at some time during their life. I have been fortunate to have had many wonderful friends, with my favorite being a black, curly haired, high strung poodle named Brandy. It was a friendship that endured for 16 years.

We first met in May, 1969 shortly after Barb and I had purchased our first home in Cuyahoga Falls, Ohio (a suburb of Akron). We had always had pets during our formative years, and had decided to purchase a pet when we purchased our home.

One Saturday afternoon, we were reviewing the classified section of the AKRON BEACON JOURNAL when we noticed an advertisement for "black, rag-mop puppies- $ 10.00". We decided to investigate, called the number listed in the advertisement for directions, and hopped in the car.

We located the address, and after inspecting the neighborhood, were not sure that we wanted to leave the warmth and safety of the car to pursue an animal. Courage replaced common sense, and we climbed the steps of the tenement, and knocked on the door of the apartment. The door opened.

Inside the apartment was squalor, and our eyes quickly scanned the furnishings, and fell upon a cardboard box. The box contained a very small female poodle, frantically attempting to nurse three tiny balls of fur.

The occupant of the apartment stated that the pups were approximately six weeks old, the mother was pedigree, and the father was a miniature poodle. I think the mother had also been stolen.

We had agreed to purchase a male puppy. Barb asked the owner if she could inspect the puppies, and proceeded to hold each of them. Finally, she held one up, and said "This is the one that I like." I asked her why she had changed her mind, and now wanted a female puppy. Barb had a puzzled look on her face. She did not realize the sex of dogs could be determined at birth. If I hadn't been along, one of my greatest friendships would not have occurred. The owner stated that the male pups were $ 5.00 each. We quickly paid, and were furnished with a Snyder's pretzel box to carry our new addition to our home.

We soon found our puppy to be very hungry, and upon close inspection, to lack teeth. Brandy was considerably younger than we had been told. We set a small platter of milk in front of him, but he was unable to lap it up. The issue was resolved when Barb disappeared to a local store, and reappeared with a baby bottle. Several times each day and evening, she filled the bottle with milk, and would hold Brandy while he emptied the contents. Brandy would sleep, at least for the first few months, in an old yellow laundry basket next to our bed. He eventually graduated to the foot of the bed, and obtained his Master's degree between us on his own pillow...only the best for my friends!

As with most friendships, our friendship had many stages, with each being better than the last. When we first met, we were both young and strong, and in perfect health. As the years took their toll on our health, we learned to appreciate our limitations, and to do things that matched our abilities.

Shortly after Brandy came to live with us, I would retreat to the basement and bounce a golf ball against the wall, and catch the carom. Brandy soon wanted to join the action, and would nudge my hand to softly bounce the ball against the wall where he, in turn, would catch the ball in his teeth.

I marveled as the ball would make a steady click against his sharp, white teeth. He was so adept at our game, and untiring. He would tease me by catching the ball, and instead of bringing it to me, would lay at a safe distance and chew on the cover. The inside of a golf ball contains rubber bands and Brandy would have them scattered throughout the basement. When the basement renovation was complete, our golf ball chasing exercises decreased.

Brandy loved to run, and we soon built a chain-link fence around a portion of our property in order to free him from the chain. He was always anxious to be outside, and he would patrol the area, sniff, and scratch when we turned him loose in the yard. Nothing escaped his curiosity. He still had a great affinity to run free.

On weekends, Barb, I, and Brandy would ride around in our car, looking for housing developments or construction sites where Brandy could run free, if only for an hour. We would throw Frisbees, sponge balls, or sticks...whatever was available. Brandy never seemed to tire, and always seemed pleased when we praised him. Brandy was always loyal, and was one of the finest friends that I've ever had. I wish everyone could have a friend like Brandy.

Brandy spent most of his day on the living room couch. From his vantage point, he could see neighbors and passersby on the sidewalk in front of the house through the picture window. His keen sense of hearing could also detect conversations outside of our front door, as well as serving as an early-detection device for unsuspecting newspaper boys and salesmen. When a strange sound occurred, Brandy would charge the front door with great speed, and leap against the door, at the same time pulling his body up the door to a height of about 6 feet.

He would catch a quick glance at the visitors who, after hearing his growl, and hearing the door slammed, would have already started a descent from the front stoop. It's strange...we had very few door to door salespeople as long as Brandy was on patrol.

When Beth was born, Brandy willingly accepted new responsibilities, including part time baby sitting duties. We also assigned him a new name. Brandy became BIG BROTHER DOG, a name that he kept for the rest of his life. He was BIG BROTHER DOG to Beth as well as David. Barb would sometimes place Beth in a playpen in the driveway outside of the kitchen window, and attach Brandy to the playpen. The children in the neighborhood would frolic with the hose or sprinkler close to Beth, with Brandy standing at attention.

He was so gentle with Beth and the neighborhood children, and put up with the abuse of being tugged at, ridden, etc. He loved children. However, if a stranger appeared, Brandy's demeanor would change immediately, especially if advances were made toward Beth, or her little friend Mimi, who lived next door. Brandy's teeth and reflexes were quite sharp by this time, partially from several years of experience catching golf balls, Frisbees and sponge balls.

His upper lip would suddenly curl up, exposing a vicious set of teeth. Most strangers would suddenly head for the front door to get approval from Barb prior to advancing to the back yard. Brandy was a loyal friend (when he knew you). In our 16 years together, he bite two people: one was a former boss (proving that Brandy was a good judge of character) and the other was a friend from our church who came in the door unannounced prior to an Easter egg hunt. Needless to say, he announced his visits after he met Brandy!

Brandy moved around the country with us, as new job opportunities presented themselves. He was welcome at most motels, and became use to fast food and travel.

The last few years of Brandy's life were not always pleasant, as his body became ravaged with tumors. His hearing and eyesight failed, and he began to walk sideways down hallways. His magnificent legs, which once propelled him to great speeds and heights, were skinny. He would lose patches of hair, and whine when it was time to go outside.

I could see him failing, but I couldn't bear to take him to the doctor and have him put to sleep. Despite his maladies, he would curl up at the foot of the bed during the day and sleep, only to rally when I opened the front door and called for him. He would stagger down the hallway, using the walls as support, and feebly greet his friend of 16 years. For such loyalty, I would carry him around the house, and up and down steps, and outside if he wanted to go.

Whenever I thought that it was time to take Brandy for his final ride in the car, he would rally and become better, if only for a few days. The will to live, which had sustained him through 16 years of catching golf balls and being a part time baby-sitter kept him going.

Finally, on a Summer afternoon, I carried Brandy to the back yard, and sat on the back step to read an article in the newspaper. Brandy wobbled around the step, and looked at me with a pair of clouded eyes. I could tell that he was in discomfort. I said to him "Big Brother, is it time to go?" Brandy crept closer, looked at me, and rested his head on my knee. Yes, Brandy was telling me that it was time to go. I started to cry because I knew that our wonderful friendship was going to end. I hugged my friend, and told him that I loved him. There was only one final act of love that I could show him, and I would do it the next afternoon.

That evening, I dug a large hole to be the final resting place of my friend. The grave was situated on a slight knoll overlooking the Muskingum River. Brandy would like it since it would receive some morning and afternoon sun. I continued to sob with each shovelful of dirt. I also coralled a knotty-pine toy box, complete with a lid and handle that I had made for Beth. I was careful that the hole was perfectly dug.

Barbara agreed to make an appointment with the vet late the next afternoon. She called me early in the morning to relay the time of the appointment. The days' activities were fuzzy…I kept checking my watch and calculating the hours and minutes until we would meet at the vet's office. Finally, the time came. I cleared off my desk, said goodnight to my secretary and headed for the car.

When I was in the car, I started the engine and removed my tie. I pulled out of the parking lot and headed for the vet's office. I began to remember all of the good things about Brandy, and all of our good times… the golf ball incidents, chasing the frisbee, his babysitting skills, our runs in the woods. I started to cry, knowing that our good times were over.

I arrived at the vet's office just as Barb was pulling into the lot. I walked over to the car, and caught a glimpse of Brandy on the floor near the back seat. He had lost his balance on the ride from home, and had been unable to climb back on the seat. Barb and I looked at each other, and she asked if I wanted her to take him in alone... I said no, and that I would do it.

I picked Brandy up in my arms in an old blanket that he preferred, and carried him into the office. His body was so light from his illnesses. I took him into the examining room where the vet was waiting. He looked at Brandy, spoke his name, and Brandy acknowledged with a slight wiggle of his tail. The vet looked at me and pulled out a syringe.

I looked at Brandy's cloudy eyes. He looked at me as he had done thousand of times before, and rested his head on my hand. In a few seconds, it was over...Brandy's eyes closed, and the vet took his stethoscope and held it against Brandy's chest. My friend was now free of pain, and in another world. There will never be another Brandy.

I quickly covered Brandy, and carried him out to the car, where I placed the bundle on the back seat. The ride home was filled with tears, as I remembered all of our good times together. When we arrived home, I placed Brandy's body, already wrapped in his favorite blanket, in a large plastic trash bag and positioned both in the toy box. I also found an old throw-rug, Brandy's dog dish, and several of his toys. I said farewell to my friend and closed the lid on the toy box, as I positioned the box in the hole. I then placed a piece of plastic film on the top of the box to keep the water and sand from falling into the cracks, and shoveled the dirt into the hole.

Brandy's grave became a special place in our yard. I planted tiger lilies and daylilies around the fringes, as well as impatiens in the Spring and Summer. Tulips, daffodils and crocuses adorned the gravesite in the Spring. I felt that Brandy's love deserved nothing but the best.

I was in mourning for several months after Brandy's death.

♡ Thanksgiving

Thanksgiving was a special holiday. Barb prepared a large dinner, and the aroma of the turkey and trimmings permeated the house. It was quite different than the antiseptic smell of the hospital. I spent most of the day on the couch, watching several of the football games. It was great to be alive, and to be home with our family and animals.

As Christmas approached, I appeared to gain strength. A good friend, a retired barber named Albert Johnson, would pick me up, and we would ride out to the mall located several miles away.

Albert was over 80 years old, an avid golfer, and a very caring individual. He would let me off at the door, and we would walk around the mall, stopping often in order for me to catch my breath. Sometimes we would browse in several stores which appeared to offer exceptional bargains. We were definitely an odd couple...an old man and a heart patient looking for bargains.

> "Make friends and you will make greater progress. The way to make a true friend is to be one. Friendship implies loyalty, esteem, cordiality, sympathy, affection, readiness to aid, to stick, to fight for. Friends are essential to success; they are still more essential to happiness. To win place, power, honor and happiness, begin by assiduously and unselfishly winning friends."   B.C. FORBES

♡ Albert Johnson

We met Albert Johnson at our church. Albert celebrated his 80th birthday when I was in Ohio State University Hospital in November, 1987. He was a retired barber, married to a wonderful woman named June, and a devoted Christian.

He stuck by our family during all stages of the transplant. He and June would ride up to Columbus in his Cadillac with Barb and I for the weekly and monthly appointments with the cardiologist. We would generally stop at the Red Lobster on the way home to Zanesville, since he loved fish.

Albert was a small man in stature, but a giant in the eyes of many people. He was generous to the downtrodden, and contributed heavily to the church, both in time and money. He was in charge of the church property, except for the flowers, which were my responsibility. Any reasonable request was filled by Albert.

He was part of a large family, and the formative years were not entirely pleasant. He was previously married, and had fathered two daughters. He had drifted into a life of alcoholism, but found our Lord. He devoted much of his life to helping others, and by serving as an example for others to follow.

When I had come home just before Thanksgiving of 1988, things looked pretty bleak. I had decided against the transplant due to the mass confusion of the evaluation process. Albert would drive his car to our home and pick me up. We would drive to the mall, and Al would walk with me around the mall, stopping often so that I could rest. We enjoyed our time together...it was quality time.

We also would stop at the local supermarket, where he would push the cart up and down the aisles. We would laugh and joke on our trips to the mall. In addition, Albert would stop at our house, unannounced, and bring oysters and other food treats for our family. He was a fabulous Christian.

When I was later a patient at Ohio State, Albert would drive to Columbus with Barb, and bring his barbering equipment to give haircuts. He also would make frequent trips to the produce section of the Big Bear supermarket to select fresh strawberries. He would take them home, and personally clean them, sending them to Columbus complete with powdered sugar.

The strawberries were such a wonderful sign of love from Albert. I will never forget how much they meant to me. Al continued to be a devoted friend after I returned to Zanesville. He would visit and bring his brightly colored sheet to spread over me as he gave his haircuts. He also helped Barb if something broke around the house...anything to make life easier for our family.

I was amazed at Albert's courage, and the example that he set for others. His spirit had helped to lift and encourage me during my hard times, and he fought with all of his strength to the end.

I spent Easter Sunday of 1990 at his home. He was bedridden by that time, and Barb and June went to church. We had a wonderful talk, and he reiterated his strong faith. I will always wonder why such a nice person had to go through such a long and painful process of suffering, but Albert never questioned his fate...I guess that I shouldn't either. I miss Al...he was a dear friend.

♡ Physical Therapy at Good Samaritan

Between October 1987 and the second quarter of 1988, I attempted to improve my physical condition by attending physical therapy sessions at Good Samaritan Medical Center. I was fortunate to meet three women who worked very diligently in attempting to help my conditioning. The women were Rhonda Forrestal, Joan Kelly, and Gretchen Tomson.

They would hook me up to the monitors, and proceed to lead me in all types of contortions on the treadmill, stationary bicycle, armagometer, and rowing machine. I found the rowing machine to be particularly strenuous, and prayed often that someone would break it in another session.

The sessions ended when my work schedule began to include a heavy amount of travel. I also has the mistaken notion that my heart trouble was in the past, and I could slack off without causing any additional damage.

After I returned home from the serious heart attack in 1988, I attempted to return to a conditioning routine. Barb drove me to the hospital, and wheeled me to the conditioning room in the basement. Joan Kelly helped hook me up to the heart monitor. I hadn't realized how my body had deteriorated during the previous two months. By the time the monitors were hooked up, I was beginning to gasp for breath, and began to feel dizzy. Joan noticed immediately, and had me sit down in the wheelchair. I felt like a total failure, and the stress of being almost helpless was hard on my ego. Certainly life was not meant to be lived like this.

♡ Transplants

The thought of a heart transplant is frightening, simply because the heart has attained a mystical connotation in our lives.

Whereas other organs such as the kidneys, liver and pancreas function without immediate attention, we immediately notice any change in the heart's function. We can feel the heart working by taking our pulses, or feeling a rhythmic beating against our ribs. The beat continues 24 hours per day.

The heart is also the glamour organ of the body. We see posters which claim "I love New York" or "I love my Terrier". Each show a heart to signify love. On Valentine's Day, we send cards to our loved ones which proclaim "I love you". The love is signified by a heart. We rarely, if ever see illustrations of kidneys, bladders, lungs or livers. We are however, inundated by illustrations of hearts.

We also know that we can function, at least on a temporary basis, if certain organs cease to function, whereas the heart's stoppage brings instant death. You have an intense fear when someone discusses the removal of the heart which has served you for over 40 years.

You enter the point of no return, since the only alternative could be an artificial heart device. At the present time, artificial mechanical hearts are not a viable alternative to heart transplants, due to risks of infection, and the ancillary equipment required to sustain the heart function. While it is possible to keep a person alive for an extended period, their quality of life is not satisfactory. You are always tethered to a set of pumps and support equipment, which limit mobility.

♡ Barb

We first met several weeks after I had graduated from the University of Maryland, and had been assigned to the general parts plant in Sandusky, Ohio. The Ford plant made vent windows, air cleaners, alternator pole pieces, and numerous other stamped, die cast and cold extruded products.

I had purchased a cup of coffee from the vending machine, and was having a discussion with a friend when she walked by the office. She was hard to miss, with platinum blond hair, immaculately styled, and an angelic face. It wasn't love at first sight, but there was definitely a strong attraction.

Several days later, we spoke for the first time, and eight months later, we were married. She likes to relate that we were not married until half time of the Los Angeles Rams-Green Bay Packers football game. Who could possibly forget those days when Travis Williams, the Arizona State kick-returner set so many records for the Packers. I noticed recently that he had died penniless, as well as homeless. It was a pity.

Barb and I moved frequently, as I attempted to find a fast track to the top of the business world. We moved from Muskegon, Michigan to Cuyahoga Falls, a suburb of Akron, Ohio and then to Ashland, Ohio.

After several years, we moved to Nashville, Tennessee and then north to Toledo, Ohio and finally to Zanesville, Ohio.

I chased a lot of rainbows, but never grabbed the gold ring. Barb and I had been through a lot together. I hadn't fully realized that the most important things in life were not one's block on the monolithic organization chart of a giant corporation, or the size of an office. I wanted to live long enough to spend more time with Barb, Beth and David.

We were growing old together. Whereas we were once the young couple with elementary school children, our kids were now in high school, and we had young friends of child-bearing age. Our looks had certainly changed, as well as many of our interests. Everyone passes through various stages in our lives...struggling to raise children...buying a home...elementary school plays...Cub Scouts...Trick or Treating...putting toys together on Christmas Eve. As I waited for a transplant, I replayed our life...the good times, and those times that were a struggle.

I had been truly blessed, with wonderful parents and brother and a devoted and loving wife of over 20 years. My children were healthy. I wanted to live longer.

♡ Decision To Seek A Transplant

I was constantly evaluating life. I looked at Barb, Beth and David and felt that I wanted to be with them as long as possible. We had always had a wonderful family, and I wanted to do everything possible to sustain the relationship.

I wanted what anyone else would want...to be able to see my daughter married...to watch my son mature, to play soccer, to drive...to spend more time with a wonderful wife who had always supported me. I only had one chance... a heart transplant.

I remembered some of the good times that David and I had spent together:

♡ David- Indian Guides

I had always enjoyed doing activities with David. After we moved to Toledo, one of his buddies mentioned an organization affiliated with the

YMCA. The organization, Indian Guides, was a group composed of many tribes, with approximately 10 fathers/sons per tribe.

Our tribe was the Arapaho, a nomadic northern American Indian tribe of Algonquian linguistic stock who had lived in Minnesota. The Indian Guides was intended to stress activities that fathers and sons could share. In addition to monthly activities and field trips, meetings were held where the boys (braves) were allowed to express good deeds. In order to speak, a wooden stick (talking stick) was passed among the braves. I was really impressed with the reverence of the ceremonies.

The activities were usually well planned i.e. trips to the post office, planetarium, Detroit Pistons basketball game, ice skating, and various workshops. We also had Spring and Winter campouts at Camp Storer, located approximately 60 miles northwest of Toledo, in the Michigan plains.

The Winter campouts were especially memorable, since the harsh Michigan weather occasionally offered challenges to non-camper types. We had a cabin which provided shelter from the elements, but fewer other amenities (such as toilet facilities).

♡ Winter Campout

During the late Winter of 1983, our Indian tribe journeyed to Camp Storer for the annual Winter campout. The fathers were prepared for the worst (we thought) and came equipped with playing cards and plenty of food to sustain us through the harsh March evening. Upon our arrival, we were directed to an isolated cabin that was clearly close to another state. The cabin was atypical of most cabins in the complex, without running water, toilet facilities, sinks, or showers. Heat was provided by a hybrid heating device which did not work.

The temperature was approximately 25 degrees when we entered the cabin. We looked at each other and grinned...we knew it was going to be a rough weekend. It was strange...the boys didn't seem to mind, and were caught up in the excitement of camping in the wild. There were about 12 of us in the cabin, and we staked out our selections of the bunk beds.

David wanted the bottom bunk, and I did not object since I was worried that he would tumble over the edge if left unattended during the evening. The bunks were noteworthy in themselves, and reeked of other Summer, Fall, Winter and Spring campouts. I later commented to other fathers that I thought every camper in Southeast Michigan had used my bunk as a urinal. It was funny...they had the same comment.

Due to the harsh living conditions, most of the fathers began a countdown to departure, when we knew that we could enjoy warm showers...and real heat. We did, however, become engrossed with all of the activities offered by the group, including horseback riding, story telling, a sing along, a tug of war, and hiking. We were, however, always cognizant of the departure time.

I was glad that David and I had gone to the local Kroger store prior to our departure, and selected a large variety of "survival food" including potato chips, corn chips, Ho Ho cakes, Twinkies, pretzels, and Pepsi... such amenities were scarce in the Michigan northland.

Several hours prior to our departure, Dave and I were walking across a wide field, on the way back to the cabin. He looked up at me and said "Dad, did you have a good time this weekend?" I said "Dave, did you have a nice weekend?". He said "Dad, this has been one of the greatest weekends of my whole life". I said "Dave, this has been one of the greatest weekends of my whole life, and I'm a lot older than you".

Dave's comment will always be very important to me, since it focused on what is really important in life...the family unit and being able to do things together. Looking back at that cold March weekend, it really was one of the most memorable and enjoyable times of my life.

Those days are gone now. David is passing through a new period of his life, the way I did and the way everybody does...he won't experience the same thrill of camping until he has a little boy of his own.

♡ Pinewood Derby

Each year, a competition was held at a local junior high school which involved a race between cars fashioned from a pine block of wood. The rules were quite simple...the Indian braves were assigned a block of wood, and were expected to carve a model race car from the block. Several weeks into the process, a double elimination meet was held to determine which Indian brave had the fastest car. Fathers were allowed to assist braves in any phase of design that could be considered dangerous i.e. the use of a power saw to craft out the initial rough shape.

I had always been lousy and non-creative with this sort of thing, and was glad that my involvement would be minimal. Dave and I went to a neighbor, a handyman of sorts, and borrowed an assortment of tools, including wood files, a power saw, drills and sanding blocks. After an initial discussion, Dave and I agreed that the optimum shape of the racer should be a wedge, with a thin front (better to reduce the wind drag). I drew several points on the block, and had David draw in the line with a straightedge. I started up the saw and cut off a sizable piece of the block. After the initial assistance, my role was limited to keeping David company, with minimal instruction regarding the use of the other hand tools.

I was fascinated by his curiosity, and the effort that he was making on his racer. He worked for hours and hours...surely his hard work would pay off with a good showing at the Pinewood Derby. Several days before the meet, another father stopped to show me his racer..what a shocker!

He remarked that he and his father-in-law had spent countless hours designing the racer for his son. It certainly looked professionally done, down to its 10 coats of candy-apple red lacquer. The father had taken advantage of his company's CAD/CAM engineering computer to design the racer. I suddenly had a terrible feeling that I had not supported Dave's effort to win the race.

I asked the father for possible tips on increasing the speed of any racer, including the placement of weights (each racer had a minimum and maximum allowance). He suggested that the million dollar computer recommended weights in the front of the car, above the front axle. I carefully weighed our entry, and found it to be light. I suggested to David that perhaps we should add some weight to the front of our wedge-shaped car. Due to the current configuration, I suggested that I drill a large hole above the axle, to insure that the hole would be straight. David concurred.

I inserted a large bit into the chuck, tightened the drill and squeezed the trigger. The drill turned, and began to bite into the front of the car... David had a bewildered look on his face (the kind of look that suggests that he's not sure if it's a good idea). He was right...it was a lousy idea. The torque of the drill broke off the front of the car above the axle, and the car was suddenly in two pieces. I looked at David...he had a terrified (and hurt) look on his face. I was terrified also.

The race was a day away, and I had suddenly destroyed my son's entry in the big event. I told Dave that I was sorry, and we would do our very best to glue the pieces together, and we could still enter the race. I prayed that the Elmer's glue would dry quickly enough (it did). The next morning, we applied another coat of silver paint to the wedge.

We went to the junior high gym about an hour prior to the race to register and scout the competition. Our entry was perhaps the plainest shaped, and crudely painted of all the entries. It was quite clear that many of the other fathers had not interpreted the rules as strictly as we had.

Our car might not have been the prettiest, or fastest, or sleekest, but we were the proudest owners in the whole race. We did manage to come close to winning our two heats, but were nosed out by the competition. Our little car stayed together...thank goodness for Elmer's glue. Dave accepted defeat much better than some of the fathers...I was proud of him.

♡ 1984 Olympic Games

The 1984 Olympic Games were held in Los Angeles. They were especially significant to the United States since our participation had been forbidden during the Carter administration in 1980.

As a prelude to the Games, a lit torch was carried across the United States by a team of runners. Most of the runners had sponsors who made contributions to the Olympic effort. Each runner carried the torch a certain distance.

I read that the path of the runners included the city of Toledo, and ascertained the day, time and street that the runners would pass through Toledo. I asked David if he wanted to venture downtown to watch the event, and assured him that the passing of the torch might not be seen again in our lifetimes. David reluctantly agreed to go.

Barb had recently returned from a trip to the Holy Land, and I wanted to have a vantage point where our new camera would best record the drama unfolding. David and I arrived early downtown, and we asked several policemen their opinion regarding angles, etc. I kept focusing the camera. Dave wanted to hold it, but I was reluctant to give it to him, since

I was afraid the strap would break, or he would be knocked down by the large crowd that was gathering.

Excitement filled the air, as a police cruiser came into view, crossing a bridge approximately one half mile away. It was leading an entourage of vehicles, including a camera crew from a major network and several official U S Olympic Committee vehicles. The cars were partially obscuring the runner, but the burning torch, and a faint wisp of smoke was clearly visible. The runner came into view, a young lady who appeared to be in her mid-twenties.

She was preparing to stop, in order to light the torch of the next runner, a young man in his late teens. She slowed down and then stopped, holding her torch against the outstretched torch held by the young man. They were standing less than twenty feet away from Dave and I. I kept snapping pictures, sure that I would have several suitable for enlarging. Dave wanted to take a few shots, and I handed him the camera. He soon disappeared into a crowd of onlookers surrounding the young lady. I waited for him to reappear, and began to worry when he did not come out of the crowd. Finally, the little blue Dallas Cowboy jacket emerged from the mob. The camera strap was around his neck.

David had a worried look on his face, and he remarked that the beeper, warning that the last picture on the film had been snapped, had not sounded. I asked him if he had dropped the camera, or if someone had jostled him, and broken the camera. I was upset, since we had witnessed a historic event, and the camera has malfunctioned. We headed for the car in order to avoid the large crowd in the area.

We found the car, and edged from the area. I was beside myself that the camera had not functioned correctly. I decided to attempt to remove the film as carefully as possible, to reduce the possibility of ruining the film. We were at a red light as I wound the levers, and opened the back of the camera. The back snapped open, and I lifted the door to expose the film compartment. I was hardly prepared for what I saw.

The compartment was empty! I had forgotten to load the camera when I took the last batch of film to the developer! I was sick...and embarrassed. How could I have been so careless? The look on David's face was priceless. He was startled. I asked him not to tell Barbara upon our arrival in Sylvania...I would tell her when she would be free to laugh at my stupidity. David agreed.

The trip home was filled with laughing. I told Dave to freeze the image of the girl carrying the torch, the camera cars, the Olympic camera cars, the lighting of the torch and the smell of the smoke. The trip seemed to out of the Twilight Zone. I was numb. We arrived at the driveway, and I again asked David to refrain from telling his mother. The car stopped, and David quickly opened his door. Barb immediately appeared at the front door.

The first words out of David's mouth to his Mom were "Mom, guess what!..Dad took a lot of pictures, but there wasn't any film in the camera!" Our secret was out. Barb had a bemused look on her face, as she fought her immediate tendency to laugh. I continued to be stunned. It was the last time that I ever left film out of the camera. As a matter of fact, I have overexposed many rolls insuring that there was film in the camera.

I also remembered some of the good times that Beth and I had together.

♡ Beth- Basketball Team

When we were living in Franklin, Tennessee, Beth expressed an interest in joining a girl's basketball team. She brought a paper home from school outlining the league rules, as well as a sign-up sheet and a section calling for adult volunteers. I volunteered to be an assistant coach. The league was well organized, and was for students throughout the county in the third through the sixth grades.

The league had been in existence for many years, and many of the girls had played for several years. The distribution of players was made through a draft. I was out of town during the week of the draft, and one of the other parents drafted the players for our team. Unfortunately, they had never seen any games, and our team ended up with older, short, "ungifted" players, and a slew of third-graders who had never played. We nicknamed the team the "Muskrats".

Our first practice was notable by the complete lack of understanding of the rudimentary rules of the game. I knew it would be a long season, and as the season began, we were routinely slaughtered (even shut-out) by the juggernauts of the league. A field goal or free throw was a morale victory for the Muskrats, attired in our little orange T-shirts.

I did the best that I could to keep the girls coming to practice, and to the games. David and Barb would come to the practices, and would bring Twinkies, Ho-Hos, and assorted pop to the practices. After the games, the girls would sprint to the concession stands for Pepsi colas, hot dogs, pop corn and candy bars. I often remarked that the girls saved their energy for the sprint to the concession stand instead of the games.

I was pleased that each of the girls displayed excellent sportsmanship, and accepted defeat and humiliation with a great deal of pride and grace. I was proud of them.

Their performance gradually improved, and the team actually won the first game of the tournament. The crowd went wild...the Muskrats had a reputation for spirited play and were a crowd favorite. The game was won when Gina, one of our Sixth graders, a rotund little girl, made a long shot as the buzzer went off. She was immediately trampled by her teammates and coach. Victory was sweet. The local McDonald's served up fries, Big Macs and shakes to a happy bunch of athletes.

Beth did not express an interest in basketball after that season. She decided to concentrate on ballet and gymnastics.

♡ Pre admission

During mid- December 1988, I was admitted to Good Samaritan Medical Center to receive a treatment of dobutimine. The drug was administered through an IV. I was very upset about being back in a hospital, since I had only been released about three weeks before from Ohio State University Hospital. In addition, David was scheduled to be in a Christmas play at church, and Barbara and I were going to celebrate our 21st anniversary.

I was depressed, and told one of the nurses about the anniversary. She evidently relayed the information to Barbara Mendleson, the head of the CCU. Within hours, my room was transformed. A cloth tablecloth was ordered from housekeeping, and put on a table in the room. In addition, Barbara and her staff ordered a cake, and champagne.

When Barbara came to visit, there were also balloons. It was the only time that we'll ever be able to celebrate in a hospital room, and again showed the love and compassion that the nurses and staff at Good

Samaritan had for Barb and I. Oh yes, I was released about an hour before David's church play. It was the nicest one that I ever attended.

♡ Transplant Miracles

When we talk of transplants, we talk of miracles, and two sports stories come to mind:

One story concerns a man named Lou Gehrig. Lou Gehrig was a famous baseball player with the New York Yankees, and is considered by many people as the greatest first baseman of all time. He set a record of 2,130 consecutive games played. He was nicknamed "The Iron Horse" because of his durability.

In 1939, Lou Gehrig made one of the most memorable speeches in the history of our country, and certainly in sport. Lou Gehrig had a terminal disease now known as ALS, or Lou Gehrig's disease. We frequently hear about the illness on the Labor Day telethon hosted by Jerry Lewis.

The speech was made in Yankee Stadium before a capacity crowd. Everyone in attendance knew that their hero, Lou Gehrig, had a terminal illness, and was near death. Gehrig gave a short speech, and closed it by saying "I consider myself the luckiest man on the face of the Earth".

What a courageous thing to say! Certainly Lou Gehrig will always be remembered as a great inspiration to our country, and to everyone who meets adversity, and who always gives their very best.

The second sports story concerns the 1980 Winter Olympic games, specifically the United States ice hockey team. The team entered a semi final game against a heavily favored team from the Soviet Union, and grabbed the lead. Surely the team could withstand the continuous assault from the Soviet squad until the end of the game. However, the game entered the final moments with the United States team ahead.

A television announcer, Al Michaels, was caught up with emotion and began to chant, as the final seconds began to count down…"Do you believe in miracles…Do you believe in miracles!" The game ended, the United States had been victors, and one of the greatest upsets in sporting history had been witnessed by millions of viewers.

The victory did not come easily to the players, and was a stunning example of tenacity...if you want something bad enough, you must expend as much energy and effort as possible.

When I think of the two sports stories, I am reminded that I consider myself one of the luckiest men on the face of the Earth, and yes, I believe in miracles.

Organ transplantation is a true miracle.

Transplant stories are full of heros, and of people who go the extra mile to help patients. Someone who never waivered in her duty was Jackie Tresl, an outstanding nurse at Good Samaritan Medical Center in Zanesville.

♡ Jackie Tresl

Jackie Tresl was a wonderful nurse. She was in her late twenties, and married to Mark, a carpenter. They lived in a home near New Concord, Ohio.

Jackie and Mark had an affinity toward animals. At one time, they rescued a young female horse that had been neglected by its owner, and gradually nursed it back to health. During this time, they felt it necessary to keep a very watchful eye on their patient, and decided to bring the horse into their kitchen. As the horse became better, she slept in the kitchen, standing on a blanket next to the refrigerator. Jackie quipped that when she and Mark had house guests, they never had to worry about someone raiding the refrigerator!

Jackie sent many cards and letters of encouragement to me while I was in the various hospitals. She was quite gifted in arts and crafts, as well as canning various vegetables. Her professional skills were also abundant, as she was promoted at Good Samaritan Medical Center.

I frequently address nursing students on the importance of people skills, and in helping patients emotionally as well as medically. Jackie Tresl had tremendous skill in being able to help mentally.

Each Christmas, Jackie sends us a card that stays on our refrigerator during the year, together with the artwork of our friends' children. Her Christmas card always has a picture of her baby...Misha the horse! She and Mark take Misha in a trailer around the county, and give rides to little children.

♡ Rita Himmelspach

I met a remarkable lady when I came to work for McGraw-Edison. Her name was Rita Himmelspach, and she retired in 1989 with 50 years of service.

When I joined McGraw-Edison in 1984, Rita was the General Accounting Supervisor at the Zanesville plant. She had a winning attitude, and was so conscientious about her job. I remarked many times, that had Rita been born a man, she would have been the President of McGraw. We spent many long hours at work when I joined the company. I was trying to get control of a multi-plant facility with numerous internal accounting problems. I had turned down several offers to join the company, fearing the commitment of top management was not strong enough to overcome the problems.

Rita was very patient with me. Her knowledge of the accounting records, as well as her insight into personnel, helped bring the mystery into clear focus. The major problems were soon identified and brought under control.

Rita celebrated her 50th anniversary with Cooper Industries (It had purchased McGraw-Edison) when I was at Vanderbilt. On the day of her anniversary, I had been notified of an impending transplant. Somehow, the news made its way back to Zanesville, and was announced at Rita's party. Evidently, the day was celebrated vigorously, only to have a letdown when the heart was damaged.

Her concern for other people helped the McGrawettes, the women's service organization of the company, consummate many worthwhile community projects. I was fortunate enough to serve in an advisory position for the organization. Janet Finley, Mildred Berry (another lady with over 45 years of service), Bonnie Bendure, Jeanette Williams, Elaine Chames and Betty Snyder all had caring attitudes and helped those less fortunate in our community.

I feel lucky to have known Rita, and to have worked with her and the ladies of the McGrawettes.

♡ Beth-Recitals

Most parents have special times in life with their children. We all have high emotions as our children learn to walk and talk and gradually gain some independence. We take great pride in their accomplishments.

Beth was especially proud of her dancing ability. Our home became a small theater, as she and her friends practiced all the latest ballet moves. The record player blared endlessly as the girls would choreograph arrangements. Our home was never as full of activity as when the dance mates congregated in the living room.

Beth's honed skills came slightly after her hopes. We went to the annual dance recital in Franklin for several years at the local high school. Beth was about 7 years old. There were about 25 acts on the program, held in the non-air conditioned auditorium.

The late Spring weather in middle Tennessee was extremely hot and humid, making the auditorium a virtual sauna. The first 10 acts went quickly, as the young people, some of them teens, danced and twirled, and jumped to the music in colorful costumes. Parents and friends were clapping and cheering the performances. I was impressed with the talent of the young performers.

As the acts continued, intermission arrived, and we ventured outside. It was extremely hot, and my clothes were soaked with sweat. So were everyone else's clothes. Had Beth already performed, I would have considered going home, as many of the parents had decided to do. We were determined to stay until the very end.

Finally, Beth's moment of glory arrived. The 23rd act of the evening featured about 10 little girls in green tights, who were going to tumble about the stage on mats. The mats were set up, and each of the performers began to tumble...some tumbled to the left, and others tumbled to the right. Some couldn't complete a revolution, and were helped by the older kids.

We cheered for Beth. She had a bewildered look on her face as she peered out into the audience, looking for the friendly faces of her Mom and Dad. I looked around. Other Moms and Dads were cheering wildly as the small people continued to roll around on the mat. What a great thrill!

The real joys of life don't consist of great honor and fame, and fortune. The things that really mean something are the things that we remember. I'll never forget the great joy of Beth on that hot, humid, Tennessee evening.

♡ Admission to Ohio State

One afternoon, in January, 1989, I called Donald Hammer, my cardiologist at Ohio State University Hospital, to see if I could be reconsidered for the transplant list. Several days later, I was approved. The wait began...I did not anticipate that it would be almost eight months and a quarter of a million dollars later before a heart would become available.

From mid January, 1989 through mid March, my condition remained stable, albeit weak. I ventured to Ohio State every few weeks to see Dr. Hammer, and waited for the beeper to go off, signaling that a heart was available for the transplant. The beeper sounded on several occasions, but they proved to be false alarms. My weight had fallen to about 170 pounds, approximately 30 pounds below the pre-illness weight. I was beginning to notice additional effort being required to accomplish tasks, with more rest being required.

On March 17, I encountered difficulty breathing and, at the same time received a call from Maggie Wooding-Scott, Dr. Hammer's assistant and one of the transplant coordinators at Ohio State. I told her of my dilemma, and she suggested that I come to Columbus, check into the hospital, and undergo some testing. It was a warm evening in March. Barb, Dave and I ate at a local steak house on the way to Columbus.

I didn't realize that it would almost be six months before I would be able to spend an evening away from a hospital again. The leaves would form and turn green, we would have snowfalls, the grass would turn green and need mowing, the flowers would bloom and Spring and Summer would pass. I would view the change of seasons from a hospital bed, tethered to several pumps and oxygen, all pumping life into my body.

I spent about ten days in the hospital, and was slated to come home on Easter Sunday. I was moved to a stepdown unit on Saturday, and was looking forward to going home. However, during the early afternoon, I developed breathing difficulties, and Dr. Hammer appeared. He ordered that I be transferred back to the CCU.

As the gurney moved into the unit, there was a flurry of activity. Several nurses appeared, and IV lines were started in my arm. Also, the transplant surgeon appeared in the doorway, and said that a trauma victim was downstairs. He said that preliminary tests indicated that the victim's heart would be used for my transplant. The doctor said he was going downstairs to conduct an additional examination and would know for sure within 30 minutes. The flurry of activity continued, with nurses continuing to draw huge quantities of blood and hooking up monitors.

I looked at Barb and Dave...they were near a corner. I started to cry. A transplant was possible that afternoon. I was afraid, knowing that it was possible that another person's heart would soon be beating in my body... if I survived the operation. What a frightening experience.

In addition to being scared, I was embarrassed that I was crying in front of my son. Looking back, it's a shame that we are raised in a culture where men are raised to hide their emotions.

I felt sorry for David. His father was crying in front of him. I remembered happier times together.

♡ David- Bill Laimbeer

One of our monthly outings with the Indian Guides was a trip to the Pontiac Silverdome to watch the Detroit Pistons of the National Basketball Association. It was during the trip that David and I met the most disliked player in the NBA- Bill Laimbeer.

Bill Laimbeer spent some of his off-season near Toledo, Ohio. His dad was a top executive with Owens-Illinois, a Fortune 500 company headquartered in Toledo. Bill once commented that he was the only player in the NBA whose father earned more than he did.

Bill's veterinarian was one of the fathers in our tribe, and he had asked Bill's wife (I think her name was Chris) if Bill could say hello to the braves if we attended a game. She thought that Bill would be delighted to accommodate our wishes.

One wintery Friday night, our tribe packed into several vans to make the trek to Pontiac, the home at that time of the Detroit Lions and the Pistons. The air was full of anticipation and excitement as we pulled into the parking lot. The Silverdome was a beautiful structure, with a seating capacity of 80,000 for football, and about 35,000 for basketball. Our seats were quite a distance from the floor, and I kidded one of the other fathers that I couldn't see the basketball court, and that nosebleed could come at any time.

We arrived early and found our seats. The boys took off to purchase pennants, drinks, popcorn and other assorted goodies. Several minutes later, a beautiful young lady, appeared in our section with an armload of Detroit Piston team posters, each autographed by all of the Pistons. What a thrill for each of the braves and their fathers.

The lady was Chris Laimbeer, Bill's wife. She told us that Bill had also made arrangements for all of us to come to the players' tunnel after the game for pictures and the opportunity to meet some of the other players.

The Pistons came from behind to defeat the Milwaukee Bucks, with Bill contributing several key free throws and rebounds at the end of the game to seal the victory. Bill's reputation as a bully was extended during the game, as he made nasty faces at the opposing players and was threatened with bodily harm by the other team.

After the game, we were ushered to a tunnel outside of the dressing room. I was talking with the boys, as newspaper reporters crowded around some of the players as they left the dressing room. Suddenly, I glanced to my right side, and noticed a giant of a person next to me...it was Bill Laimbeer.

He looked much larger than his program dimensions of 6'11" and 250 pounds. Perhaps his college weight was being used. He extended his right hand, and introduced himself...he had the biggest hands that I had ever felt. My extra large hands felt so small, as I was dwarfed by this man.

I don't want to ruin Bill Laimbeer's reputation as the most aggressive, nastiest player in the NBA, but for a few minutes, he was a considerate, gentle person. He had his picture taken with each of the boys, as well as several group shots. He was very patient, despite a busy schedule.

I'm sure that he was anxious to go home, and to find peace for the duration of the evening. If anyone happens to see the Pistons in person, please cheer for Bill Laimbeer...there are some Indian Guides who consider him to be a hero.

♡ No Transplant

Several minutes passed. The nurses left the room, and Barb, David and I all hugged each other. We were not sure how much longer we would have together. Several more minutes passed. The transplant surgeon, P. David

Myerowitz, appeared in the doorway. He stated that he had examined the heart, and that it had been damaged during the accident. There would be no transplant on Easter Sunday.

Days soon turned into weeks, and weeks into months without any transplant activity at Ohio State. I was told that other transplant centers were encountering similar experience with a slow down in activity. One thing was sure...the lack of donors nationwide was causing the unnecessary deaths of 1/3 of all heart transplant patients on waiting lists.

During the long wait at Ohio State, I met a man from West Virginia, who was also waiting for a heart transplant. He and I became good friends during the long wait.

♡ Jimmie Taylor

I met Jimmie Taylor while I was a patient at Ohio State University Hospital during the Spring of 1989.

Jimmie was 36 years old, married to Kathy Taylor, and the father of two teenage sons. He was from a small town near Parkersburg, West Virginia.

He had experienced a heart attack in February, 1989 at his farm, but the extent of the heart damage had not been determined. However, extensive examination at Ohio State revealed substantial damage that could not be corrected through normal surgery. His only chance of living depended upon the heart transplant option.

Jimmie was one of the nicest people that I have ever met. He enjoyed farming, especially as it related to raising cattle. He had the strong calloused hands of a farmer.

He was not an educated man, and remarked on several occasions that during his high school courtship with Kathy, it was she who had prepared all written, take home assignments. He did, however, converse easily with both his friends and strangers.

Jimmie was proud of his hunting exploits. He often staked out strategic locations in a "holler" near his home during the Spring and Summer months in order to maximize results during the deer and turkey hunting seasons. He was proficient with a rifle as well as a bow and arrow, and taught his sons to respect the destructive power of weapons.

Jimmie waited until mid-June for his transplant operation. During his wait, he and Kathy occupied a small efficiency apartment near the hospital. He would call me at least once each day, and would never fail to come to the CCU when he was in the hospital for blood work or other appointments. He and Kathy made the most of their time together, although they were restricted by Jimmie's physical limitations.

They obtained fishing licenses and visited the Columbus zoo. In addition, they enjoyed television, playing cards and discussing their future back at home. Jimmie was anxious to see his many calves, and to assist with the harvest of hay.

Several days before I was transferred to Bethesda Hospital in Zanesville, I attempted to call Jimmie and Kathy at their apartment, but there was no answer. I became worried that something had happened to my friend. Finally, I heard that Jimmie was in the hospital, and was being prepared for a transplant. I asked to see him, as I wanted to wish him the best of luck, but was told that it would be impossible.

There were some complications in procuring the heart, so the actual operation took place the next day. Kathy and Jimmie's mother came to my room for a short discussion. We all prayed for a miracle...our prayers were answered when Jimmie woke up with a new heart, beating vigorously with the gift of life. The news of Jimmie's opportunity was wonderful to me, since Jimmie had become like a brother during our long wait together.

I had the opportunity of seeing Jimmie within 48 hours of the operation. He was sitting up in his bed, and gave the thumbs-up sign when he saw me. It was one of the happiest moments of our lives.

Jimmie made good progress with his new heart, although he did experience some complications which forced him back to Ohio State for treatment. Generally, his heart biopsies had been uneventful, with each success bringing continued optimism regarding the future. Meanwhile, he was able to return to his home near Parkersburg, supervise one of the hay cuttings, and ride an ATV to see his baby calves. His dreams of a normal life were being realized.

When he and Kathy would travel to Columbus for his biopsies, they would go out of their way to visit me at Bethesda Hospital. At the end of August, he and Kathy stopped for a quick visit. Several weeks before, I had kidded Kathy about the home-made preserves she had made for the physicians at Ohio State. They had a wonderful surprise ...they brought a jar for me.

I was taking physical therapy when they visited, and was discouraged...I had been in various hospitals over 5 months waiting for a transplant. I was on the exercise bike, hooked to the IV pumps and the central oxygen supply. My future was bleak. I decided to try to qualify for the listing at Vanderbilt University Medical Center.

Jimmie sensed my discouragement, and seemed sheepish, almost apologetic about his healthy condition. He grabbed my arm, and from beneath his blue surgical mask, said that he loved me, and never to give up. His eyes displayed love, and his tears displayed the deepest type of sincerity. We hugged each other. It was the last thing that we ever said to each other.

Several weeks later, I was able to go home prior to the trip to Nashville. I was on the patio when Barb appeared at the doorway, closed the door, and came out to sit with me. She had received a call from one of the transplant coordinators at Ohio State with information about Jimmie Taylor.

He had contracted a virus, and had experienced breathing problems. He was on his way to the operating room for testing when he expired. A very good friend, who had provided love and encouragement during some dark hours, was gone. I will always have a place in my heart for Jimmie Taylor...I'm sorry that he's not here any more.

♡ Beth's Visits

Beth would drive to Columbus on her off days to visit me in the CCU. We had had many interesting experiences together.

♡ Teaching Beth to Drive

One of the milestones that we as parents pass, is the ritual of teaching our children how to drive. Beth represented a significant challenge to Barb and I as she reached the age of negotiating an automobile about the roadways of Muskingum County. The citizens of our county were not aware that Beth would be turned loose on unsuspecting motorists.

We did everything right (we thought)...we enrolled Beth in a driver's education class at her high school, and were extra careful when she was in the car. I took her to Dillon State Park, near Zanesville, in the fall where we endlessly cruised the parking lots and back roads.

We would practice...forward...backward...turning right...turning left...turning on directional signals...emergency flashers...starting and stopping and parking. We practiced and practiced. I thought we were prepared for any contingency. Even the rides home on the highway were preparation for the test, although, at 35 miles per hour, several motorists became quite annoyed at us.

I must admit Beth was not the best student. Her attention span seemed to ebb and flow, and each week, as I had her slide behind the steering wheel of the family car, she would ask me the same questions. She would adjust the seat as well as the inside and outside mirrors, and secure her seat belt. She always asked, "Now which pedal is the gas and which is the brake?"

Barb become nervous riding with Beth, and eventually assigned all teaching lessons to me. One afternoon, Beth wanted to drive into Zanesville, so she and I requisitioned the older of the family cars, a 75 Chevrolet nicknamed "The Beast" for the short trip into town. We drove down Dresden Road, one of the busier roads leading to town, and turned onto Taylor Avenue. I immediately noticed that Beth, in her haste to make a quick turn, had driven onto the sidewalk. She didn't notice the car was riding higher on the passenger side than the driver's side, and she seemed quite pleased that she was closer to her destination.

I asked if she noticed anything different about how the car was driving...she didn't. I asked if she noticed the road felt bumpy...she didn't. I asked her to stop the car, as I noticed the car was about to become impaled upon a tree stump. Beth stopped the car, and suddenly noticed the tire marks on the grass. I think she was careful, and gave pedestrians the right-of-way after that incident.

Beth's driving was always a concern for her family. She later ran into a stone wall in our new car (she forgot which pedal was the gas, and which pedal was the brake) and later tore the front fender off "The Beast". She has been driving for three years since the incident with "The Beast" and has not had an accident with her own car.

Perhaps all daughters should have gifts of automobiles on their 16th birthdays, in order to save the family cars.

♡ Learning to Drive

The memories of teaching Beth how to drive brought back memories of my first car. I lacked common sense, and perhaps Beth's driving habits were an improvement over my youth.

♡ The Bomb

Most of us have a car during our lifetime that has special meaning to us. The car with the most memories for me was a 1954 Ford convertible, purchased in 1959 with earnings from my first Summer job.

I had a job in a boatyard during that Summer, and the major duties included the scraping of barnacles from the bottom of yachts and painting the bottoms with anti-fouling paint to prevent additional barnacles from accumulating. The paint was especially nasty. My base pay of $ 1.00/ hr. netted about $ 29.00 each week, the majority set aside into a savings account.

Toward the end of the Summer, Dad and I began to research the classified section of the newspaper to find a car, specifically one to replace the 1953 pink Studebaker as my major type of transportation.

One Sunday, we happened to spot a 1954 Ford convertible, painted forest green with a black top. The car had a small V-8 engine, with straight shift and overdrive. It seemed like the perfect car, and we bargained the owner down to $ 600.00. The purchase immediately cleaned out my bank account.

The next day, I noticed that the spare tire was flat, and the top would not raise up easily, once it was down. Dad suspected that the mileage was understated on the odometer, and our good deal was not such a good deal after all.

I was sure that we had located all of the serious shortcomings of our purchase. I went out to start the car, and was met by a groan. Dad made a few adjustments, and the engine started up immediately. I had a date that evening with my steady girlfriend, but Dad cautioned me against taking the Ford, since he was going fishing that evening and would not be available for mechanic duties should something happen to the car. He suggested that I take the 1953 pink Studebaker.

Dad went fishing. I took one look at the Studebaker, and immediately headed for the Ford convertible. It was a hot, humid evening, and what better way to spend time than in a convertible with the top down? I would throw caution to the wind, and take my chances with my new purchase. When the evening unfolded, I found that I should have listened to Dad.

My girlfriend and I went to the movies and afterwards decided to park for a few minutes at our favorite spot, located on one of the fairways of Annapolis Roads Country Club. It was a mistake, especially with the new car. The young lady was supposed to be home at midnight, so about 11:45 I turned the key and waited for the roar of the engine. Instead, I heard the terrible groan noise.

This was serious. Dad was fishing, my date had to be home in 15 minutes, and I had no idea how to start the car. We were in the middle of nowhere, and it was pitch dark. We didn't have a flashlight either.

We listened until we saw a car and walked to the road, and began to follow the road until we found a house with a light on. Finally, about 1 a.m., we approached a house, knocked on the door, and were greeted by a sleepy looking gentleman, who graciously allowed us to use his telephone. We placed 2 calls...one to Barbara Ann's mother...and the other to Dick Hines, my boss and next-door neighbor.

I called Dick because I thought that he would be home, and be sympathetic to my problem. Since Dad had specifically advised me not to take the Ford convertible, I didn't think that he would cheerfully come tow us home.

Dick Hines was familiar with the area around the golf course, and asked specifically where the car was located. Since I had never been on the course during daylight hours, I couldn't give him a specific direction, or hole. We agreed to meet him on the entrance road.

About 45 minutes later, I spotted headlights slowly approaching on the access road. It was Dick, and he never looked better. We located the derelict vehicle, and he attempted to start it, having only as much luck as I had experienced...in other words...NONE. He eventually attached a tow rope to the front bumper, and we began the long trek back to Arnold, stopping first in Annapolis to take Barbara Ann home.

At about 3:30, we finished pulling the car back into our yard. I quickly checked...Dad was still fishing. Since I knew what Dad's reaction would be should he learn of the incident, I asked Dick if he could keep a secret until the following week. Dick was a good friend. It wasn't until 20 years later that Dick told my Dad of the daring rescue from the golf course.

Several years later, the Ford began to show its age, and maintenance costs suddenly became excessive. I sold the car to a friend for a low down payment (a mistake) and three monthly payments, none of which were ever received. Finally, Dad and I repossessed the convertible. It had been seriously abused by the new owner. We decided to refurbish it.

I took off some of the chrome, sanded the body, and took it to Earl Schieb, world renown for their $ 29.95 paint jobs. Our forest green car became white. I also replaced the black convertible top with a new white vinyl top, and new throw seat covers put on to cover the rips in the seats. We bought spinner hub caps for the front wheels, and spun aluminum moon hub caps for the back wheels. I added seat belts for the front seats.

The biggest change concerned the engine. We located a 1957 Thunderbird V8 engine with a 4 barrel carburetor that delivered close to 300 horsepower. We added dual glass pack mufflers that delivered an ominous sound at red lights, and were especially noticeable during early morning hours. The car became known around our house as the Bomb.

The Bomb was a lot of fun. I suppose that if David were to ask for a similar car today, I would have serious problems providing him with one, since I had many harrowing experiences with the Ford.

One experience concerned a drag race with a friend whose Dad had given him a new Chevrolet Corvette.

I was at a party one evening when my friend started to belittle the Bomb. After many insults, I showed my immaturity (and stupidity) by challenging him to a race on Route 50, a major thoroughfare which is close to Annapolis. We decided to race near the Severn River Bridge. We waited on Route 50 until we could not see any traffic heading East. The race started, and the speedometer was soon showing 80, 90 and 100 miles per hour.

We approached the bottom of the bridge, and I literally put my foot in the carburetor. The speedometer hit the post at 110 miles per hour, and we were still accelerating...the glass packed mufflers changed pitch as the Bomb began to pull away from the Corvette. I finally became scared and backed off of the gas. In a few seconds, the Corvette went by, and almost seemed to ramp at the crest of the bridge. The Bomb was drifting between the lines, and the wind was whistling through the vinyl top. I kept watching my friend as he got to the end of the bridge, still doing about 120 miles per hour. In a minute I noticed another thing...a blue swirling light from the roof of a state trooper's car.

My friend had not noticed the policeman waiting near the foot of the bridge as he went screaming by. I tooted as I passed my friend, who was occupied in removing his driver's license from his wallet as I went by. I didn't know what a charmed life I was living until the next morning, when Dad commented that one of my bald tires was flat. Had the tire blown out during the high speed race the previous evening, I would have been crab bait in the Severn River.

♡ Beth- Hair

Beth was always cognizant of the latest fashions, trends and hair styles. I was never in tune with fashion, and had my hair cut at Noll's Golden Comb, close to McGraw-Edison in Zanesville. Fred Noll, the barber, charged me $ 4.25 to shorn my locks. Needless to say, Fred concentrated on speed.

Beth was always experimenting with different styles and colors. One day she would be a blond, and the next day, a brunette. Her bangs would be visible one day, and be gone the next day. I often wondered how other parents were able to keep up with the endless changes of young women.

I found out my tolerance level one afternoon, when Beth had an appointment at the mall cosmetologist. I dropped her off one afternoon, and agreed to pick her up later in the evening. When she called, darkness had invaded the afternoon, and I caught a glimpse of her before she sat in the car. Something looked strange, and I thought my eyes were deceiving me. Another look confirmed the first impression. Beth's hair was multi-color! Red on the sides, yellow in the front, and green and black on the top. I asked her who was going to pay for the work. She said I, of course, and by the way, how did I like it.

I told her that she looked like a stoplight. The stony silence lasted several days after the next day, when she returned to the hairdresser for a conversion back to the human race.

I look back at the incident and wish that I had been a bit more tolerant of Beth and her hair styles. Perhaps as we have experiences near death, the whims of teenage girls do not seem to be very important, at least to us.

♡ Waiting at Ohio State

The three months of waiting at Ohio State University Hospitals seemed like an eternity. Transplant activity had nearly stopped, with the latest transplant being in mid-February when I entered in mid-March.

The bright spot every day was the receipt of mail, which usually brought a plethora of cards from church friends, including drawings from Sunday School classes. My folks, brother, friends at Cooper Industries, and numerous aunts, uncles, and cousins kept the mailman busy delivering words of encouragement.

The evenings and nights brought a great deal of anxiety. Since most traumas occur during evening hours, I was always waiting for the transplant staff to appear at the door with news of an impending operation. Except for the false alarm on Easter Sunday, I was never prepared for another operation at Ohio State. I was in the Columbus CCU for three months.

The physical discomfort occasionally became a problem. The numerous IVs required to administer the solutions rendered the arm veins almost useless. The nurses would sometimes require seven or eight sticks in order to find a suitable vein. Many times, the vein would collapse, and the fluid would infiltrate, collecting in the surrounding tissue causing swelling and stinging. My forearms would bulge with the accumulation of fluid. The process of finding another vein begin again, with additional urgency, because termination of treatment caused extreme risk.

The veins located in the arms, hand and wrists became useless due to the deterioration. The attending physicians decided to install shunts to carry the fluids to the heart. The procedure was performed in the room, with a sterile field made possible by draping sheets over the body. After a local anesthesia was administered, an incision was made in my neck.

The process was not comfortable, and was performed each week during the wait at Ohio State. The level of skill exhibited by the person performing the procedure varied widely.

I also wondered about the rotation of staff, although it is a common practice in teaching hospitals. The beginning of each month brought a new staff composed of an attending physician, resident, intern and student. The juggling of the staff does not bring a great deal of comfort to a long term patient, with new personalities and treatments with which to become familiar.

♡ Bad Evening

I had many uncomfortable evenings, with one evening particularly disconcerting.

I usually stayed up until midnight watching the television news. Some evenings, I experienced breathing difficulty, due to the accumulation of fluid in my lungs. The problem is a symptom of cardiomyopathy, where the heart is not able to provide ample blood supply to the body. The short term solution to the problem is to take several diuretic pills, called lasix. When I felt the problem developing, I rang for the nurse to request a dose, and since the problem was common, I was not overly concerned. I informed the nurse the problem was not severe. She listened to my chest, and left the room to obtain approval from the night physician before administering the drug.

Several minutes later, a doctor appeared in the room, together with several interns and students. They each took turns listening to my lungs, and proclaimed I had an accumulation of fluid in my lungs. He agreed I needed a diuretic, but was not going to prescribe the medication.

Instead, he was going to find out <u>why</u> the fluid was accumulating. I became quite upset because he ordered numerous tests, most of which were not necessary. I knew why the fluid was accumulating..the heart was beating at a low efficiency. The crew watched as an EKG was administered, chest X-rays were taken, blood draws were made and a blood-gas test was taken from my wrist.

I was concerned that the costly tests were being made unnecessarily, and without regard to cost. Finally, the doctor prescribed the diuretic. I thought the episode was the biggest waste of insurance possible, since the tests were ordered by someone completely unfamiliar with my condition, without consultation with the attending physician. My pleas for reason were completely ignored. As I look back at the incident, the funds spent during that evening were paid out of my diminished resources, since later testing was funded from personal assets when the insurance expired.

♡ Hospitals

We are very fortunate in the United States to have excellent health care facilities. During the long wait for a transplant, I spent many months in various hospitals.

♡ Sheri and Dawn

The nurses at Ohio State University were caring professionals. Two of the nurses stood above the others. Their names were Sheri and Dawn.

Dawn was a tiny single girl (she has since married) who had graduated from nursing school in Columbus, using funds set aside by her grandmother. Her grandmother, upon her birth, saved $ 1.00 each day and presented the money to Dawn upon graduation from high school.

Sheri was a petite redhead who was raised on a farm. She was married to a young executive, a former Air Force Top Gun candidate, who worked for Blue Cross in Columbus.

I became very familiar with both of these young ladies during my three month internment. In addition to working the same shift, Dawn and Sheri were close friends away from work. Many of the actions taken to help me during the period were jointly planned.

One action involved a picnic in my room. One Sunday afternoon, they took away my lunch and told me that they had planned a surprise. I didn't know it at the time, but they had also consulted with Barb in planning the picnic. I looked up and found both women carrying picnic baskets, filled with a checkered tablecloth, place settings, and all types of foods and vegetables...a real feast! Barb and I never ate so good or probably ate as much as our picnic in the CCU unit.

Dawn was always concerned about the sunshine, and wanted me to be able to enjoy sunny days, even when it was cloudy outside. One morning, she came into the room with a pair of scissors and several sheets of construction paper. She proceeded to cut out a sun, complete with rays and attached them to my window. This simple act of kindness brought many happy hours during the stay.

Sheri and her husband probably went out of their way more than any couple that I met during my illness. There were occasions when Sheri would travel into the hospital during her days off to take me outside to sit in the sun. One of the most relaxing things for me while in Columbus was to be transported to a courtyard in front of the hospital. Unfortunately, two people were required to accompany me, and attend to the paraphernalia, which included two IV pumps and an oxygen bottle strapped to the pole. Most of the time, the staff was unable to find available time, and I understood the time constraints. Sheri and Greg appeared frequently to assist me with my wishes. I think we are all lucky in this world to have such wonderful young people. I knew that they had something better to do on Memorial Day than to wheel the wheelchair and pumps down to the courtyard...at least more fun.

After I transferred to Bethesda Hospital, the caring did not end. Dawn and Sheri came to Zanesville and visited me while I was in the CCU. They came armed with fresh fruits and vegetables, as well as Cracker Jacks and other assorted goodies. I felt honored then (and still do) that they would take time off from their busy schedules to provide encouragement.

♡ Spouses and Families

The pressure and uncertainty on the families of transplant patients are immense.

While I was in the hospital, Barb continued her hectic schedule...rising early, working until the afternoon and commuting daily to Columbus, with a return to Zanesville to be with our family and more work at home. The following day brought more of the same.

The pressure on the spouse of a transplant patient exceeds the pressure on the patient, since both are subject to the same uncertainties and the spouse has other problems and uncertainties regarding the family at home. The spouse is torn between their own needs, the needs of the patient, and the other family members at home. The spouses are the unsung heros in the transplant stories, the least understood and the least appreciated. Attention is constantly being focused on the patient, while the spouse receives only the overflow.

♡ David Strickler

During the three month wait at Ohio State University Hospitals, we learned that cancer was ravaging the body of David Strickler, Barb's father. His illness increased the stress on Barb, as she watched disease gradually destroying both her father and her husband.

    Her parents lived in Sandusky, Ohio home of Cedar Point Amusement Park, on the shores of Lake Erie, a drive of about 3 1/2 hours from Columbus. She was cautioned by the transplant staff against traveling to Sandusky, since my condition was tenuous, and the travel would put her out of range if a heart became available. Finally, her Dad's condition became more critical. He had been moved back to his home. Barb received a call from the visiting nurse, who advised that the end was near.

    I urged her to make the trip to Sandusky, and she, David and Beth made the journey to visit her Dad. He was in good spirits when they arrived, as he marshalled his resources in a courageous reflection of strength. They had a good visit, although my family was shocked by how the dreaded disease had ravaged his body. His body had deteriorated and the treatment had caused his hair to fall out. His spirits were good, and he was glad to see them. Several days later, Bob Strickler left this earth. His nurse commented that it was a miracle how he had hung on until his beloved daughter and two oldest grandchildren had visited him.

    I was deeply saddened by Mr. Strickler's death. I felt so hopeless, since I couldn't attend his funeral. I wrote the eulogy, which was to be read at the service for a man that I had respected for well over 20 years. He had been a loyal and devoted friend, father, son, grandfather, husband and brother. I tried to capture the essence of his life in his eulogy.

♡ David Strickler Eulogy
Written By John Garrett
May 28, 1989

We are here today to honor and remember David M. Strickler Jr., who entered our world on February 10, 1923 and entered our Father's world on May 27, 1989. Mr. Strickler was sixty-six years old.

    Many people leave legacies. David Strickler's legacy will not be a monument which can be measured by its breadth, its depth, its width, or its ornateness. He will not leave a fortune to be distributed to charities.

His legacy will be greater than monuments and grander than money. His legacy will be a memory of him, of how he lived and loved, and an example to his wife, his children, his grandchildren, and his great-grandchild.

Mr. Strickler will be remembered as a man who loved and honored his wife of 47 years, Betty; his children, Barbara and Jim; his daughter-in-law, Kathy; his son-in-law John; his grandchildren, Beth, David, Leta, Heather, and Jason; and his great-grandson, Tony. He also cherished his brothers, Jerry, Claude, Harry and Jake, and his sisters, Dorothy and Wilma. He will also be remembered as an uncle, as a loyal and devoted friend, and a master to his dog Yogi.

What type of man was David Strickler? He had many nicknames, including Bob, Hank, Stub, Gampa, and Daddy. David Strickler was not complex...he led a simple life. He loved John Wayne movies, television game shows, card games, and sports, especially the Indians and the Browns. He loved to pitch horseshoes and go to reunions. He was a Navy veteran, a member of the Fraternal Order of Eagles, and the United Auto Workers.

He always gave his best effort. He worked at Ford Motor Company and rarely missed work. He worked when he was ill. He worked when the snow was deep, and when the weather was oppressively hot. He took pride in his work and in his company. Bob Strickler had pride...he had integrity and was always honest and loyal.

Bob was always available to help others; the young and the old, relative or friend, anytime during the day or night. He gave to everyone and asked for nothing in return. His wants were simple...to sit in his rocker/recliner, a cold beer, a warm cup of coffee, and the presence of his wife and closest friend, Betty.

What are some adjectives to describe Bob? Warm, kind, gentle, sharing, caring, loving, loyal, understanding, hard working, supportive, concerned, helpful and patient.

As we spend a final hour with Bob, let us recall that the world was bettered by his presence. He is now with our Father in heaven. We thank the Lord for putting Mr. Strickler on His earth, and we will always remember him.

♡ Emotions

I encountered the entire gamut of emotions prior to the surgery, especially while waiting for the transplant at Ohio State University Hospital. The emotions ranged from sobbing to euphoria. The long hospital internment created many periods of hopelessness, as hours turned to days, days turned to weeks, and weeks into months. The lack of transplant activity, the escalating cost of hospitalization, and the emotional strain on my family created constant worry, frustration and pressure. The coping with factors beyond your control causes terrible psychological problems.

♡ Helicopters

When you are waiting for a transplant, there are occasions when you hate your own reactions to certain events.

I noticed the most dramatic change when viewing the television news, reading the newspapers, and listening for the Life Flight helicopters. Prior to being a transplant patient, I was always concerned with the well-being of trauma victims, specifically those involved in motorcycle, and auto accidents as well as gunshot victims. I didn't want anyone to die, since I knew that total families were affected (mothers, fathers, children, etc.). We all place a premium on the sanctity of life. Life is precious.

I went through a period where I felt guilty, when a helicopter would arrive at the hospital. I would wonder if the occupant was critically ill, and if they would become an organ donor. I would wonder about their blood and tissue type as well as their size and weight. Also if they had signed a donor card. I knew that if I were to live, someone else would have to die.

I felt like a lousy Christian. I prayed for the victims, and prayed that God's will would be done.

♡ Support from Friends

I received many cards and calls from friends during the long months in the hospital. The encouragement from one friend, Bill Tschudy, had special meaning.

"The friend who can be silent with us in a moment of despair or confusion, who can stay with us in an hour of grief and bereavement, who can tolerate not knowing, not curing, not healing, and face with us the reality of our powerless, that is the friend who cares."

HENRI NOUMEN

♡ Bill Tschudy

I first met Bill Tschudy when we were working for a large defense contractor in Toledo, Ohio. I was employed as a Manager of Cost Accounting, while Bill was a Marketing Manager.

Bill had an engaging personality, and we became friends very quickly. We often had lunch together at a Chinese restaurant close to the plant, and our relationship was similar to that shared by brothers.

One afternoon, another employee mentioned that Bill was a war hero. I found the comment strange, since I had known Bill had been in the armed forces, but he had not mentioned any extraordinary experiences.

Bill had, indeed, been a war hero. During the beginning of the Viet Nam War, Bill was a navigator on an aircraft shot down by a surface to air missile. The incident was later portrayed in a movie entitled When Hell Was In Session and concerned the aircraft's pilot, Jeremiah Denton, who was later to become an Alabama legislator. Bill and Denton successfully parachuted from the aircraft, although Bill suffered a broken back. Bill commented that when he was floating to earth, hundreds of small Asian people, many brandishing machetes and bamboo poles appeared below him. He thought they would attempt to decapitate him.

The flight to earth began an incarceration of over seven years and seven months. Bill was moved frequently during the first several years, and was regularly beaten and abused by his captures. He spent the last several years at the Hanoi Hilton. When a settlement came to the conflict, Bill's likeness was on the cover of Time Magazine. Bill's faith in God and the love for his family sustained him during his long captivity. I asked him why he never gave up. Bill replied that he knew that God would not let him die, and his country would come and rescue him.

Bill would frequently make patriotic speeches to schools and groups near Toledo. His deep faith in the United States were an inspiration to anyone who heard or knew him.

I often thought of Bill during the long wait in the hospitals. Whereas he had been tortured and starved, I was very lucky. I had a clean bed to sleep in, television to watch, and meals available during the day. My family and friends could visit, send cards, and call. I had many people attempting to keep me alive.

I often heard from Bill. He had a new job which took him to the West Coast, and he would frequently call while he was between plane connections. I also received many cards and notes, imploring me to press on, and never to give up. It meant a lot coming from Bill, since he personified courage and tenacity of the highest order. Bill would also call Barb, and was always willing to extend a sincere offer to help.

Bill and I still correspond or call each other frequently. He has a devoted wife, Janie, as well as a son, Michael who will soon graduate from Ohio State University, and a daughter, Nancy, a high school student. They live in East Aurora, a suburb of Buffalo.

I feel so very lucky to have Bill as a friend. He has enriched my life.

My brother Joe kept trying to rally me during the wait.

♡ Joe- Calls at Ohio State

Joe called me at least four times each week when I was waiting in the various hospitals, without fail. I don't think anyone could have been more loyal during the endless wait. Even if he and Carolynn went on weekend trips, the calls continued to come. Joe was trying to rally his brother, just as he had many times before.

At the beginning of June, I requested a transfer to a local hospital in Zanesville, and was assured that my position on the national priority listing would not be changed, as long as I was kept in a CCU, and was receiving IV solutions. I was in a weakened condition...my weight had dropped to 146 pounds, and I was unable to find strength to exercise.

No transplants had been done at Ohio State since Valentine's Day due to a lack of donor organs. Although I had been notified that several hearts were available, one donor was suspected of being on narcotics, and another was from a donor who had been terribly obese, with resultant arterial damage.

♡ Zanesville

Our family lived in Sylvania, a suburb of Toledo, Ohio from the Summer of 1981 to the early Summer of 1984 when I was working for a major defense contractor. The company manufactured turbine engines for the cruise missile.

I had originally been hired by the Controller to modernize the financial reporting system, and had made significant progress during the first two months in identifying the major weaknesses of the current methods.

One day, the Controller did not come to work, and I heard that he was having heart problems. Information regarding his status was limited to only his closest, long term friends.

The Controller, a vibrant man in his late 40's, never came back to work, except for a few hours one Saturday to pick up some personal effects. I saw him in the hallway, and was astonished by his emaciated condition. He had lost so much weight, and his eyes were sunk back into his head. I gave him a big hug, and wished him well.

Several weeks later, he died. Although I never learned of the exact cause of death, I heard that his malady was inoperable. Perhaps a heart transplant, if more popular in 1981 could have prolonged his life. I lost a good friend when John died.

I eventually located a position with McGraw-Edison, a manufacturer of electric transformers for the utility industry. Our Product Line was headquartered in Zanesville, Ohio with other manufacturing locations at Nacogdoches, Texas Visalia, California and Lumberton, Mississippi. We eventually closed the Visalia facility, and opened a parts plant in Matamoros, Mexico. McGraw-Edison was purchased by Cooper Industries of Houston in 1985, and provided a stimulating and challenging environment.

The position in Zanesville offered a unique opportunity to live and work with an extraordinary group of people. I was discussing Zanesville one afternoon with someone from Columbus, and the visitor asked if there were any surly people in Zanesville. They had been to Zanesville on many occasions, and had never met anyone who was not completely honest and open with them. I commented that our family had lived in many communities around the country, and we had never seen so many nice people per capita.

Zanesville is located in the South central part of Ohio, about 45 miles east of the state capital (Columbus) and 65 miles west of Wheeling, West Virginia. It is a typical small (28,000) town with a single newspaper (The TIMES RECORDER) a Television station (WHIZ-TV) and a mall on the North part of town. The teenagers congregate at the mall on the weekends, and drive up and down the main drag (Maple Avenue). The major employers are the two hospitals.

At one time, Zanesville had a significant industrial base, but eventually many of the potteries in the area closed due to the pressure of exports, and unemployment rose as coal mines ceased operations. Even McGraw-Edison saw an exodus of jobs to Mexico and other locations. Many of the citizens of the county began to anticipate the worst of conditions, and many were not disappointed. Relocation of other industry to the area was slow. I often wondered why a more concerted effort was not made to promote the virtues of the town, including proximity to a large metropolitan area, good transportation and an ambitious and capable workforce. Zanesville became caught up with finger-pointing, and eventually began to believe the awful things that they had been told. The education standards in communities began to slip, as levies were continuously defeated. The talented young people of the town have begun to leave.

Zanesville is a town of caring people. I noticed a closeness immediately upon the beginning of my employment with McGraw-Edison. There was a pride of workmanship in the factory, and a sincere sense of cooperation in the office workforce. When I became ill, I was besieged with hundreds of get-well cards from salaried and hourly personnel, together with cards from neighbors, people from our church, and many other churches in town. I taped many of the cards on the walls of my hospital room, and visitors were amazed at the quantity and variety of cards.

The people of Zanesville have a deep interest in the issue of organ donations. I am frequently asked to address church groups and schools in the area and spread the word about the "Gift of Life". The audiences are always receptive. I wish there was more that I could do to curb the exodus of jobs, and to help our community.

The media in town is always supportive of worthy causes. The local radio station (WHIZ AM/FM) was recently presented with an award which is given to only 10 stations in the United States for community service. The program manager of the station, a dynamic young man named Pete Petoniak, helped to develop numerous public service announcements that were broadcast throughout southeast Ohio.

The station also was a joint sponsor of the March of Dimes Cake Auction, which raised more money for the March of Dimes than any similar event in the United States. The enthusiasm of the management and staff of the station brings much good to the community.

The local newspaper, the TIMES RECORDER is similarly community minded. During my illness, frequent updates chronicled my progress, as well as the need for increased donor awareness.

♡ Transfer To Bethesda

I was transported to Bethesda Hospital in mid June...what a great feeling to be close to home! Our friend Jan Tandy brought our brown dog, Samantha, to the emergency room door. Samantha sniffed, I kept talking to her, and she suddenly realized that her master of four years was laying on the stretcher in front of her. Samantha was overcome with emotion. Her tail began to wag feverishly and she began to wine and yip. She rolled on her back, still yipping, and nudged my hand toward her belly. I scratched her...we were both in ecstasy. I remembered when Samantha and I had first met. It was after Brandy had died.

♡ Samantha

Barb had mentioned that she felt David was ready for a dog of his own. Since Brandy had lived with us for so many years, and was full grown when David was born, he was never considered to be their own dog. Each week, Barb would ask if it would be OK if she and Dave made a trip to the animal shelter to find a new dog. Finally, I gave my consent.

One morning, she advised me that she and Dave were going to stop at the Muskingum County Animal Shelter, and look for a replacement for Brandy. She asked if I wanted to be part of the selection committee...I said no, since our new pet was to be David's dog. Our only input was that we wanted the new dog to be smaller than Brandy, suitable as a lap dog, but other than size, the decision would be up to David.

Later that morning, Barb called and reported that Dave had fallen in love with a female beagle, and asked if I wanted to come to the shelter for the final approval. I again declined, but was pleased with Dave's selection. I looked forward to meeting our new addition later that evening.

When I pulled in the driveway that evening, David rushed to the car with his new sweetheart. She was a beautiful brown and black dog, but it was obvious that her heritage had been seriously misrepresented to Barb and Dave. She had beautiful brown and black markings, but her feet were quite large. I knew that she would eventually mature to somewhat larger than a beagle. Dave named her Samantha Julie, a feminine name for a gentle lady.

Samantha displayed a vociferous appetite almost immediately. Her visits to the vet confirmed my suspicion that her ancestors were not to be confused with great hunters, and she eventually grew to about 65 pounds. She also displayed a curiosity for the unknown, and successfully escaped from her makeshift pen several times, before her girth reduced her ability to squeeze through various openings. Her complete gentleness was in stark contrast to Brandy's high strung attitude. Her demeanor was easily influenced if we displayed any favorable or unfavorable response.

Ironically, several years later, Barb and Dave noticed another female dog with markings identical to Samantha. The owner remarked that his dog, Sandy, had been adopted from the Animal Shelter within a week of Samantha's adoption. Apparently, they were from the same litter, and had been dumped on a country road, and brought to the Shelter by a passer-by. Sandy also displayed ample girth (approximately the same size as Samantha) perhaps proving that eating habits are probably hereditary.

Samantha's gentleness is one of our finest gifts. As with many animals, a dog's soothing demeanor can work wonders for their owners during periods of anger, worry or depression. We, as humans are lucky to have pets as therapy for our everyday problems.

I often wonder how people can be mean to God's creatures. Certainly, we can not be kind to each other until we find peace with animals.

♡ Transfer to Bethesda

My Zanesville cardiologist, Dr. Brian Jones, had a look of disbelief when he looked at me that afternoon. My condition had deteriorated. I often wondered whether I could, in fact, have survived a transplant operation in my weakened condition.

Dr. Jones stated that he expected me to exercise, and to eat as much food as possible, as often as possible, and whatever I wanted to eat. He said that I could eat Chinese food, potato chips, French fries or pickles. Dr. Jones felt that everything possible should be done to put on additional weight. He indicated that I would soon be able to begin an exercise regimen. I was somewhat skeptical...I felt so weak, and could not imagine climbing on a stationary bicycle and exercising for 30 minutes.

Dr. Jones was right. Within a few days, I began to have more energy, and was consuming large quantities of food and fresh fruit. The kitchen at Bethesda was very responsive to my needs, and would send extra helpings of fruit, chicken or anything available to cure the insatiable appetite.

At one time, the dietician came up to the room for a visit, looked at me, and had a bewildered look on her face. She had heard about the patient who had been eating double meals, fruit plates and Chinese food, and wanted to see this large person. She was expecting to see someone who tipped the scales at about 300 pounds, and was surprised by the 146 pounder laying in front of her. We had a good laugh together and the extra helpings continued.

The physical therapy sessions began. A family friend, Sonie Mathews, worked in the physical therapy department and would roll a wheel chair up to the room several times each week to pick me up. Sonie was a tiny lady, an avid jogger, and a caring person. She would hook up the pumps and oxygen to the wheelchair, and we would head for the elevator for the trip downstairs. The wheelchair and I probably weighed twice what Sonie weighed, and was, at times, quite cumbersome. Sonie never complained... we were both on a mission.

Once in the exercise room, Sonie would hook up the oxygen supply to a wall unit, position the pumps next to a stationary bike, and help me on the bike. She would monitor the activity of the heart from a console. Gradually, the 30 minutes of activity became a wonderful diversion from the waiting for the call from Ohio State. In addition, Bethesda provided some small dumbbells to use while lying in bed. I would do 500-1000 repetitions per day in an attempt to strengthen my arms.

♡ Information From Ohio State University

The call from Ohio State University Hospital notifying me of an impending transplant never came. After a month at Bethesda, I was becoming very discouraged at the lack of transplant news.

About this time, a friend from Nashville, Al Smith, talked to Barbara regarding the apparent lack of progress in obtaining a transplant. He had recently read an article in the Nashville TENNESSEAN regarding the transplant program at Vanderbilt University Medical Center. The article had chronicled the 50th transplant, and mentioned the average wait as being 4 weeks. I thought the article was a misprint.

I decided to call Vanderbilt. I talked with Faye Johnson, the secretary in the transplant center, who advised that the article was now outdated. In the few weeks after the article, other transplants had been performed, and yes, the waiting list was about 4 weeks.

♡ Al Smith

Al Smith provided the initiative to pursue a transplant at Vanderbilt University Medical Center in Nashville.

We had been good friends since we had both worked at Aladdin Industries in Nashville, beginning in 1978. I was in Finance and Al was in charge of the plastics manufacturing and mold shop. We were both imports...Al was originally from the Boston area and I was from Maryland. We hit it off immediately, and we took an interest in each other's perspective of the business.

Ironically, we both left Aladdin within several months of each other in 1981. He and his wife Mary started Almar Molded Products in Nashville, a custom plastics molder in Nashville. I have always felt a measure of pride in Al's company, since I had a small part in its original operation. Al and I jointly developed data related to the pricing of his products related to the application of factory overhead.

Our friendship continued as I moved to Toledo Ohio, and later to Zanesville. We would discuss certain business alternatives, and I guess that I provided a good sounding board for his proposals. Al made a lot of good decisions. His business today is very successful, despite many sudden economic ebbs and flows during the last ten years.

When I became ill, Al would frequently send cards, or call, or talk with Barb and offer his total commitment to our family. He became quite alarmed when the wait for a donor heart became longer and longer. When I left Ohio State University Hospital and transferred to Bethesda Hospital in Zanesville, Al became more determined than ever to help our family. His calls and cards became even more frequent.

During one of his discussions with Barb, he asked if we had ever considered Vanderbilt University Medical Center for a transplant. He had read an article in the TENNESSEAN, the morning Nashville newspaper, regarding Vanderbilt's 50th heart transplant. The article also stated that the average wait for a transplant was four weeks. Al wondered if I had thought of coming to Vanderbilt. He discussed the article with Barb, and sent it to her.

♡ Follow-Up

The article prompted many calls to various agencies and hospitals. It was during this time that I was told that I was no longer on a priority listing. I had spent many weeks waiting for a call which would never come.

Dr. Jones asked what I wanted to do, and I stated that I still wanted to live, and to pursue a transplant. He agreed to do anything in his power to certify me on another listing. It was a promise that he spent countless hours and effort in achieving...without Brian Jones, I would not be alive today. The complete staff at Bethesda Hospital was intent on helping us to achieve our objective.

♡ Race to Qualify for Another Program

I could hardly believe the information. I decided to call other hospitals around the United States, including Johns Hopkins in Baltimore, the University of Maryland, St. Thomas Hospital in Nashville,

Presbyterian-University Hospital in Pittsburgh, and several other hospitals. I obtained survival rates, waiting list totals and listing requirements.

UNOS (United Network of Organ Sharing) in Richmond Virginia was established in 1986 to act as a clearing house nationally for organ transplant programs, and to insure that abuses in the transplant programs were eliminated.

♡ Selection of Vanderbilt

After additional evaluation of statistics, we decided to attempt to become part of the listing at Vanderbilt University Medical Center in Nashville. Vanderbilt had an excellent success rate, one of the most active programs in the United States, and was led by Dr. William H. Frist.

Dr. Jones contacted Dr. Ted Eastburn, a cardiologist at Vanderbilt who screened most candidates. Dr. Eastburn agreed to consider me for additional evaluation. Dr. Jones forwarded results of tests performed at Bethesda Hospital to Dr. Eastburn, who reviewed the results, and agreed to have me come to Vanderbilt for additional testing. We were very appreciative that Vanderbilt would give us additional consideration, since my heart was continuing to labor very inefficiently.

The next obstacle concerned the transportation to Nashville, with many alternatives considered. Sue Little of the Social Services Department at Bethesda pursued many possible solutions. Each possibility presented a formidable obstacle. Transportation aboard a commercial airliner was ruled out because they would not let anyone aboard with IV pumps. Travel aboard a military aircraft was ruled out due to the irregular schedule and a space available policy.

Arrangements were finally made with Southeastern Ohio Air Service to provide the use of a private aircraft for the flight to Nashville, Tennessee. The cost of the flight was borne partly by the air service, and Bethesda Hospital. Bethesda also provided the services of Phyllis Lake, one of my favorite nurses to accompany us on the flight. The trip to Vanderbilt would be Phyllis's last day at Bethesda, since she was leaving to get married. The trip was scheduled for the Wednesday following Labor Day.

I was spending time at home, waiting for the trip to Vanderbilt. It was during this time that I heard that a good friend, Jimmie Taylor, had died from a virus which had attacked his transplanted heart. I was looking forward to the trip with mixed emotions, since I was saddened by Jimmie's death but knew that Vanderbilt was my only hope to live.

♡ Support from Pets

During the long tenure at Bethesda Hospital, Samantha and Susie would visit me when I was having physical therapy. Barb and Sonie Mathews would arrange to bring the animals to the physical therapy room. What a great thrill to have them among the whirling, spinning sounds of the stationary bicycles and other exercise equipment.

♡ Susie

During the Spring of 1987, we had encouraged David to participate in some type of public service for the community. The suggestions included serving lunches in a hot meals program, serving as a volunteer in one of the local hospitals, or perhaps to assist at the Muskingum County Animal Shelter.

Since Dave had adopted Samantha at the shelter, he felt an allegiance to other animals, and began to volunteer on Sunday afternoons. His tasks included cleaning some of the cages, as well as taking many of the animals on short walks on the road leading to the shelter.

One Sunday, David's social schedule developed a conflict, and he commented that he was going to cancel the work at the Animal Shelter. I immediately discussed the commitment that he had made when he consented to volunteer, that the other volunteers depended on his help to take care of the animals, and that the animals looked forward to their walks and deserved clean cages. Although my arguments made sense to me, David felt his most recent commitment was more important. I gave him permission to take the day off, but decided to take his place as a volunteer for the afternoon.

When David had volunteered for his duties, we had told him that we did not want him to become attached to any of the animals, since our home was already the residence of Samantha and Natasha, Beth's cat. We knew the adoption rate for the animals brought to the shelter was quite low, despite the dedicated efforts of the employees to find homes for the animals. The workers at the shelter supplied unbounded love to the animals brought there, but severe space limitations made euthanasia necessary for most of the animals. David had a clear understanding of the agreement.

I reported to the shelter that afternoon, and volunteered for any assignment that the supervisor wanted me to perform. Fortunately, some other volunteers had begun to scrub each of the 14 cages, most of which were filled with at least one large dog or several smaller pups. There was a constant din, as each of the animals expressed their personality to the workers.

The supervisor gave me a choker collar and leash to walk the dogs, and I started down the row of cages. There was a mixture of dogs, ranging from a German Shepherd, who was blind in one eye to several small pups of mixed ancestry. I felt an attachment to each of the animals, as we walked down the hot, dusty road. I knew that many of the animals would not be adopted, and would be put to sleep if homes could not be found for them. I talked to each of them as we stopped in order for them to sniff the trees and grass next to the road.

Their tails wiggled and wagged as the kind words were spoken to them...they were appreciative of the affection directed to them. What a shame that their love would be neglected by most people. I was sorry that I was not rich enough to provide a home for them until they were adopted, but I did want to make a few minutes happy for them.

One of the cages contained a tiny black female with spindly legs. Each time that I went to her cage, she ran through an opening leading to the outside. I eventually completed the round of cages except for the little black dog, and asked one of the teen workers if they would help to corral the scared animal. The young lady commented that she felt that Sadie May, the name given to the dog, was afraid of me because I was wearing a baseball cap.

It seems the animal's owner had been wearing a baseball cap when he discarded her at the Animal Shelter, and she had been abused. I took off the hat, and my new friend and I walked down the lane. She was very inquisitive, stopping often to sniff the grass. She kept looking up at me, and I noticed that one of her eyes was crossed. She was not one of the most attractive dogs available for adoption, although she was special. I completed the rounds, making sure that each of the animals had been out of their cage.

During the week, I often thought of that Sunday afternoon at the Animal Shelter. Three of the dogs were imbedded in my memory...the blind German Shepard...a beagle named Sounder...and the little black female dog. I decided to discuss a possible addition to our family with Barb. She agreed to go to the Shelter with me, knowing that we really did not need another animal.

When we arrived at the Shelter, we ascertained that the German Shepard had been put to sleep during the week. We went to Sounder's cage, and he yipped and barked and jumped against the door of the cage. Barb and Dave felt that Sounder was better suited for country living than as a house dog. We were drawn to the cage of Sadie May, who was sitting passively against the side of her cage with a bewildered look on her face. She stood up quickly and backed up as I began to talk to her, and I noticed that I had not removed my baseball hat...she was frightened.

We discussed Sadie for a minute, and agreed that since we already had a female dog, we would concentrate our efforts toward a male dog during the following week. I left the building, and walked to the car, thinking of the blind German Shepard's fate. Barb remained in the building talking with the supervisor. David remained at the Shelter to perform his weekly duties.

When we started the trek home, I noticed that Barb was quite emotional, and we began to talk. She had discussed Sadie's history. She had been brought to the Shelter three months before by a man wearing a baseball cap, and driving a pickup truck. She had obviously been kicked and abused, and was undernourished. Her life had not been easy, and she had been an exercise in survival.

The personnel at the Shelter had done everything in their power to help her become adopted, including a picture and article in the local newspaper. The publicity had brought a lot of activity, and one family had taken her home, only to return the next afternoon because she was too hyper. Other potential families dismissed this cross eyed, skinny dog because she wasn't very pretty. The personnel felt that she was adoptable, but they couldn't keep her any longer...this was to be her last week at the Shelter.

Barb asked if we could give her a chance. I consented to bring her home, but would consider adoption only if Samantha, our previous refugee from the Shelter, would share her home graciously. We both felt an obligation to help this animal who had been locked up for over three months. Barb drove back to the Shelter to bring back the frightened little dog.

When Barb returned home, we opened the back door, and Samantha came charging out. We released the little black dog, and they examined each other. After several minutes, their tails wagged, and they began to play. It was the start of a beautiful friendship, not only for Samantha, but also for me.

We renamed our new charge Susannah Jane, and began to call her Sue. As time went on, Sue began to gain confidence in her new environment. She was very attentive to me, especially if I kept the baseball cap removed, and we became special friends. If I went to the basement to start the woodburner, Sue would follow. Whenever I would move about the house, Sue would follow. She loved affection, and always greeted us with a chorus of barks when we arrived at the house from visits to the grocery. She and Samantha immediately became acclimated to each other, and enjoyed frolicking about the house and in their backyard. Others may have felt that Sue was not very pretty...I found her to be beautiful.

I am so happy that I substituted for David at the Animal Shelter, because I was able to meet my sweet Sue.

♡ Bethesda Nurses

I left Ohio State University Hospital in mid June and transferred to Bethesda Hospital in Zanesville. Bethesda Hospital was about one mile from home, and was a homecoming of sorts. I didn't know much about the hospital prior to the transfer, but soon encountered additional nursing professionals who "went the extra mile" to help.

The supervisor at Bethesda was named Becky Leasure. Becky was a pretty lady in her late 30's who scheduled the nurses in a manner to minimize any disruption of my care. My condition was tenuous, to say the least, and my weight was approximately 146 pounds. I had weighed over 200 pounds prior to the illness.

Phyllis Lake was one of my favorite nurses. She was always very supportive and available to discuss almost anything that was troubling me. She would later play a large role in two of the most important events in my life...my daughter's wedding and the airplane ride to Nashville to qualify for the transplant list at Vanderbilt University Medical Center in Nashville.

♡ Beth's Wedding

Barb came to the hospital one afternoon, and told me that Beth and Thuy wanted to get married. I accepted the news with mixed emotions...Beth would recently turn 18 years old, and, as our own lives have shown, the world offers many experiences for those who wait.

On the other hand, I knew her imminent marriage may have been my last chance to walk her down the aisle. Every father harbors a desire to give his daughter away. Beth seemed to be deeply in love. She had dated Thuy for over three years, and he had been her only serious boyfriend. The wedding was set for several weeks in the future.

I notified Dr. Jones of the marriage, and asked him if there was any way that he could arrange for me to give my daughter away. After considerable thought, he said he wasn't sure, but he would do everything possible to fulfill my wishes. He immediately began to search for various alternatives, and remarked that I might be the only father to arrive for a wedding in an ambulance. Everyone in the hospital worked together, and finally Beth expressed a desire to become Mrs. Thuy Luu in the chapel of the hospital. Dr. Jones, the nurses, the pharmacists and other personnel made arrangements to facilitate the wedding.

The nurses would navigate the wheelchair to the chapel for dry runs. Dr. Jones and the pharmacists made arrangements to obtain portable pumps that fit into the pockets of my suit coat. Extra oxygen was ordered, and placed in front of a chair in the chapel. A family friend, Gretchen Sayre, tailored my suit pants to allow for the 60 pounds that had been lost since the illness began. The nurses in the unit also helped decorate my room for a reception for Barb, Beth, Thuy and I following the wedding. A small cake was ordered, and Gretchen made some of her secret punch.

The days prior to the wedding were long, as I worried that I would not be able to participate in the wedding. Finally, the day arrived.

One of my nurses, Phyllis Lake, surprised me that afternoon. She had made arrangements with her daughter to bring a striking change of clothes to wear when she rolled me to the chapel, complete with high heels and jewelry. She looked gorgeous, just as she would later when she accompanied Barb and I on the flight to Nashville a month later.

When we arrived at the chapel, the local newspaper was there, together with Jeff Donahue, from the Public Relations Department of Bethesda. Jeff had written an article for the local newspaper that became a front page story the following morning.

Phyllis pushed the wheelchair to an alcove where Beth was waiting. She looked beautiful in her dress. She reached for my hand, and I began to cry. I told her how happy she had made my life. I had reached a milestone despite unusual circumstances. We talked for a minute, and Phyllis pushed the wheelchair to the doorway. I disconnected the oxygen, and Phyllis helped me stand up. The tape recording of the bridal march had already been played. Someone signaled to play it again. I listened for the music. It began again, and Beth and I started down the 15 steps to the front of the chapel. I could feel the tears welling up in my eyes.

The wedding was emotional. When I returned to my seat, I immediately hooked up the oxygen, and began to cry with tears of joy. Barb handed me a handkerchief, and sniffling could be heard throughout the room. It was one of the greatest moments of my life. I had achieved one of my goals in life...to walk my daughter down the aisle.

After the ceremony, Beth, Thuy, Barb and David came to the CCU for cake and punch. I laid in the bed, taking an occasional picture of the newly married couple and feeling happy to be alive.

♡ Wait at Bethesda

The wait continued at Bethesda, as Dr. Jones worked with the staff at Vanderbilt to attempt to have them qualify me for their listing. During that time, interest in transplants in Zanesville increased. Several newspaper and television interviews ensued. I was happy that the subject was gaining additional publicity, since the increased interest might lead to additional public awareness.

♡ Suicide

The evenings spent waiting for the transplant varied, with some evenings filled with anxiety. Others were filled with hope.

While I was at Bethesda Hospital in Zanesville, I would sometimes venture to a bench located outside the emergency room, usually after midnight when activity in the CCU calmed down. Due to the pumps and apparatus required to keep me alive, one of the nurses would accompany me, usually pushing a wheel chair.

The time spent outside was wonderful, and the nurses and I had profound conversations. I looked forward to being outside, even tethered to a pole receiving IV drips and oxygen.

One particular hot and humid evening stands out from the rest of the nights. Grace Barnhart, one of my favorite CCU nurses, and I had spent about 20 minutes outside when we heard an ambulance siren in the distance.

Suddenly, the doors of the emergency room opened, and three or four hospital personnel came running through the doors, pushing a gurney. The siren of the ambulance came closer to the hospital, and was turned off as the vehicle entered the grounds of the hospital. The ambulance entered the circular drive leading in front of the emergency room. The ambulance pulled in front of the emergency room doors and stopped. A flurry of activity ensued.

The back doors of the ambulance burst opened, and the driver quickly opened his door and ran to the back of the ambulance. The emergency room attendants quickly approached the back of the vehicle. My view became temporarily blocked by the large group of medical personnel attending to the patient. A few minutes later, the gurney was removed from the ambulance and placed on the ground. The patient was not doing well.

As the wheels of the gurney were extended, I noticed the patient. He had a tube extending from his mouth, and a stream of blood had tricked down the side of his face from his ear. I assumed that he had been in an automobile accident. The flurry of activity that had accompanied his arrival ceased. I asked Grace to help me back to the room, since the sight of the injured man was not a pretty thing to watch.

During the early morning, I learned that the young man had found life to be filled with unresolved problems, and who felt the only way to find peace was to take his own life. He had taken a revolver, placed it against his head and pulled the trigger. Death was instant. He had been found by his family, who immediately called the rescue squad. Despite the heroic efforts of the personnel, the young man's life had ended.

The incident occurred shortly after Beth's wedding in the hospital chapel. My plight had been stated on the first page of the local paper, and the young man's family asked if his heart could be used for a transplant for me. The heart had deteriorated during the attempts to save his life, and other problems, including differences in blood and tissue type and my removal of my name from the transplant list (without my knowledge) prevented the transplant.

The young man's family consented to donate virtually all of his other organs and tissues, either for transplant or medical research. I often think of the large number of people who were able to benefit from the tragedy which occurred on that hot, humid evening. The gift of life had been received from a stranger, for the benefit of many others.

♡ Bethesda Nurses

The nurses at Bethesda did everything to make my stay as painless as possible, and went the extra mile on many occasions.

Several weeks after I was admitted, Grace Barnhart asked if there was anything she could do to make my stay easier. I mentioned that I was concerned that Barb's birthday was fast approaching, and I had not purchased a card. The next evening, Grace was scheduled to be off work, and I was surprised as she entered my room. She and her daughter had gone card shopping, and she was carrying several cards for me to choose. She had gone the extra mile on her day off. Grace also brought sweet corn and other fresh vegetables to the unit for me to enjoy.

Carolyn Winland and her husband frequently had cook-outs at their home. On several occasions, they would cook extra portions of food, and bring the meal to the unit on the following morning. After Dr. Jones gave the approval of any food, Carolyn and Reg would cook bratwurst and bring it to the unit.

Shelley McPeek helped make arrangements for Beth's wedding in the chapel at Bethesda. She frequently wheeled me down to the chapel to look at the seating arrangements, and accompanied me down the hall to take showers. She also brought her children to the hospital for me to meet. She later transferred to the physical therapy department at Bethesda, where she works closely with Kerry Green and Mary Kitzig.

Michelle Lemmon was a striking, blond nurse who originally had her picture taken with me shortly after my arrival at Bethesda. Several of my former cohorts at McGraw-Edison commented that they knew why I didn't want to get out of the hospital, since Michelle was taking care of me. Michelle was single and loved Chevrolet Corvettes. Her mom, Pat, worked in the maternity unit at Bethesda, and took care of Beth and Sebastian when he was born.

Alyson Yusufzai was married to a physician, and had two children, a son and daughter that were the same ages as Beth and David. We spent many hours together, and talked of many experiences. She had lived in many places around the world, and our discussions were varied. She wrote many letters and cards to me while I was in Vanderbilt, and gave me a book <u>Everything I Need to Know I Learned in Kindergarten</u> on the morning of my flight to Vanderbilt.

Shortly after I arrived at Bethesda, I broke a tooth eating some coffee cake. Since I was not able to leave the hospital, several dentists were requested to come to the hospital. Alyson was very diligent in tracking down someone brave enough to work on a transplant patient. Several dentists would not come, but Alyson was vigilant and persistent. The dentist, Eric Cromwell, with his wife as his assistant, diligently completed the repairs in the room, despite the IV's and the oxygen being administered simultaneously. Alyson was, and continues to be a loyal friend.

Jim and Lisa Oakley were a married couple, with both working as nurses. Jim and I had frequent discussions concerning business. He was very interested in computers. Since I had some experience at McGraw-Edison, I encouraged him to continue with his night school classes. I found him to be very well rounded, and am sure he will be a success in any field that he chooses.

Carol Johnson, Cindy and Dan Smith, Cheryl Roller, Theresa-,

MaryAnne Johnson and Lauren -----, and another married couple, Pete and -------were also instrumental in helping me to survive until the transfer to Vanderbilt.

Annette Warheim, a young nurse from Coshocton, was always a joy. She always insisted in calling me Mister, even when I asked her to call me John. She was engaged to a long distance truck driver. I always kidded her about the wild experiences that long distance truck drivers had in far away cities. Annette still sends me cards and notes. She still isn't married... maybe I scared her away from the truck driver!

♡ Rain

Many of us have experienced extended periods of confinement, and have yearned to be outside. For most of seven months, my only taste of the outside environment consisted of short trips to benches, when nurses were available to assist me with the IV pumps.

When Dr. Jones permitted me to come home (prior to the trip to Nashville), I wanted to sit on our covered patio if we had a thunderstorm. I wanted to hear the rain beating against the roof, to smell the rain as it hit the warm sidewalk, and to hear the thunder and see the lightning.

I was lucky...several days later, a severe thunderstorm passed through Zanesville, and the rain falling on the corrugated fiberglass had a soothing effect upon me.

As we rush through life, we should appreciate all of the things that God gives to us. Since the operation, I've heard some people complain about the weather, but I've learned that there are no days that aren't beautiful.

♡ Cooking Out

I've always enjoyed cooking outside on a propane grill. Like most backyard chefs, our family moved up from a small, round charcoal grill (took forever to heat the coals) to an electric grill (limited range, but with lava rocks) to the current model with two burners. What a beautiful smell to have the smoke blowing about the neighborhood...a sure sign of Spring and Summer!

During the internment at Ohio State University Hospital, and Bethesda Hospital in Zanesville, I craved food cooked on a grill. Occasionally, one of the nurses or Barb would bring a treat to the hospital, but something was missing. The smell of the smoke, the sizzle, the constant flipping of the lid and adjusting the flame.

One of the great joys in eating grilled food is the love in preparing it. I missed the opportunity from March 17 through April, May, June, July, and most of August. Thanks to Dr. Brian Jones, and the staff of Bethesda Hospital, I had the opportunity to go home during the end of August. One of my objectives was to cook on the grill, perhaps for the final time. I was determined to find a way, despite the pumps, the tubing and the oxygen. We succeeded.

Everyone thought it was a crazy idea, and several friends offered to come over to our home to grill the food, but it wouldn't have been the same. I knew that we could find a way.

I asked Thuy, our son in law, to carry the pole and pumps to the patio. I drug the oxygen tube through the sliding glass doors, and hung the cannula on a nail. I lit the grill, hobbled back to a chair, grabbed the oxygen tubing and took a deep breath...it would work! The process was repeated again and again as the chicken gradually cooked. What a great thrill to be able to accomplish something that most people would take for granted.

That evening, I felt euphoria as we ate our meal.

♡ David's Soccer Game

I had missed many of David's soccer games during the various illnesses, and was determined to attend another of his games prior to the trip to Nashville. Dr. Jones and the staff at Bethesda Hospital had gone the extra mile in making provisions for me to spend some time at home prior to the testing at Vanderbilt. I was still on the two IV pumps and the oxygen supply when I went home.

David's team was slated to play a home game several days before I was scheduled to leave for Nashville. I told Barb that we were going to the game. She looked at me in disbelief, and said that it would be impossible. I asked her to call Janet Bone, David's soccer coach, to see if we could park close to the field. Janet felt that arrangements could be made to accommodate our wishes.

We had several items to attend to, with the two IV pumps, and the oxygen supply being the most critical. I asked Thuy to carry the IV pole to the garage and place it next to the car. I sat on the back seat, and had Thuy disconnect the IV pumps from the pole. I sat the pumps on the back seat, and hung the IV bags on the little hooks where you would normally hang clothes hangers. We put two small bottles of oxygen in the back floor and connected one to the cannula. I also brought along a urinal.

We arrived at the field, and took our position which offered a good view of the field. We did, however, cause many heads to turn as many people noticed the apparatus hanging in the car. The trip was a success… David's team was victorious, and we had accomplished another triumph, major in our eyes but perhaps minor by other standards. I had cried during the game, since I was both happy, and also apprehensive that I had seen his last game.

♡ Trip To Nashville

On the morning of the trip, Anne England, a family friend, and the wife of Bob England, came to the house in her van. It was a beautiful morning as we carefully loaded the apparatus into the van, being careful not to pinch any of the tubing. We were all nervous, knowing we were coming closer to our objective. We pulled out of the driveway, and I took a final look at our home. I wasn't sure if I would ever see it again.

The trip to the Zanesville Municipal Airport took about 20 minutes. We passed the spot where the heart attack had occurred, on Interstate 70 East of Zanesville. We stopped at the red flasher, close to the fast food restaurant where the pain had been so intense, and I had asked God to spare me. It seemed so long ago. So much had happened…the long stays in the hospital, the endless pain and testing, the emotional roller coaster, the death of friends. I was anxious to bring the result to a conclusion.

We pulled onto the tarmac, and I noticed many familiar faces. Grace Barnhart, one of the nurses at Bethesda, and her husband Mark had come to say good-bye. Alison Yusufzai, another nurse and a terrific person, had come bearing a book <u>All I Really Need To Know I Learned In Kindergarten</u> which provided many hours of enjoyable reading at Vanderbilt.

The anchorperson, George Hiotis, at the local television station WHIZ-TV, and a cameraperson were also on hand. George and I had a short interview. He asked me how long I would be in Nashville. I told him that I was cautiously optimistic, but the stay could only be for a few days if I was not accepted into the transplant program. He wished me well.

Bethesda Hospital had provided corsages for us and the reporter from the local newspaper took several picture of us as we boarded the plane. The door finally closed. We fastened our seat belts, the twin engines roared into action, and I took another look at Zanesville as the plane quickly gained attitude for the two hour flight to Nashville.

Arrangements had been made for an ambulance to meet us at a private hangar at Nashville International Airport. As the plane landed and taxied to the hangar, we could not see a medical vehicle. Evidently, the change in the time zone had not been discussed or calculated in the arrangements. I did see our old friend Al Smith, who had sent the original article concerning Vanderbilt's transplant program to us. Al quickly walked to the plane, and had a shocked look on his face when he looked at me. It had been seven years since we had seen each other. I was about 60 pounds lighter than he had remembered and my complexion was pasty. We shook hands, and we hugged each other. Al was very nervous as he asked when the ambulance was coming to take me to the hospital.

Summers in Nashville are oppressively hot and humid, and we arrived during a warm afternoon. The heat was intensified by the asphalt. I began to have breathing problems, and everyone grabbed a pump and we staggered into a lounge in the hangar. Al and I talked as we waited for the ambulance. He would take Barb to lunch, and over to Vanderbilt while I was being admitted. He was obviously nervous, but relaxed when the ambulance arrived.

The ambulance was supposed to have a nurse to accompany me to Vanderbilt, but the medics had come alone. Phyllis Lake would jump aboard the ambulance, and ride into the hospital. It seemed so fitting... Phyllis and I had done a lot together. She had accompanied me to the chapel at Bethesda Hospital in August for the marriage of our daughter

Beth, and spent many hours with each other as we waited for a decision from Vanderbilt.

The trip to Vanderbilt was slow, as we hit the mid day traffic. I became nauseous as the ambulance wound its way to the emergency room. I noticed familiar sights out of the window...I felt like I was home. I was apprehensive upon returning to the city that had been our home eight years before. I felt that I would either die in the city, or gain a renewed life.

♡ Vanderbilt

The first evening at Vanderbilt was depressing. I was hooked up to a hard monitor, which limited my mobility to just a few feet. After having spent ten days at home, during which I had gone to a soccer game and cooked on a grill, the confinement was a mental shock. I called Barb, who was staying at our friend Peggy Buchanan's home, and sobbed.

She assured me that things would soon be better, and that the personnel at Vanderbilt wanted to be more familiar with my condition and requirements. She was right. The next day, I was moved to a step-down unit, and outfitted with a mobile monitor. I could walk the halls, pushing the pumps and oxygen supply and getting some exercise.

The first evening, I also met Ted Eastburn, the cardiologist who would conduct the various evaluations. Ted was a laid back guy, who wore his hair pulled back into a pony-tail. Debby, the nurse who checked me into the unit, had mentioned that Ted often conducted his hospital rounds in blue jeans and Western shirt. When I met Ted, I was taken by his engaging and confident personality, and how easily he laughed. As our relationship lengthened, his sincerity and empathy for his patients became even more evident. Our clinic appointments are something that I look forward to each quarter. When we see each other, it is almost as if we have never left each other.

The first week at Vanderbilt was filled with many tests. I was impressed by the efficiency and professionalism displayed by the personnel. I was pleased at the most menial things for a large hospital, including the housekeeping.

♡ Beverly Walker

Several days after admission to Vanderbilt, I was visited by Beverly Walker, a transplant coordinator. Beverly was a tiny lady, friendly and bubbly, with an engaging personality.

Beverly was also very intelligent, having obtained a Master's degree in Nursing. Her soft Southern accent was very comforting to Barbara and I.

We discussed my physical condition, and the need for continued physical rehabilitation sessions. We concluded that additional sessions should be conducted at the Kim Dayani Fitness Center, located in a separate building from the hospital. We agreed that she would schedule a session in several days. Beverly agreed to transport me to the center in a wheelchair.

On the day of the session, we were met by a typical Nashville summer day...the kind that I refer to as a 190 day i.e. 95 degrees, with 95 % humidity. Beverly came up to the room, and was able to find a pole with good wheels. She attached the pumps to the pole, strapped a small oxygen bottle to the pole, and propped me comfortably into the wheelchair. Our journey began.

Beverly pushed the wheelchair to the elevator, through the hospital corridors, past the various clinics, cafeteria and offices. We came to the doors leading to the street, and were met by a burst of oppressively hot, humid air. It felt like a blast furnace had been opened on our faces. We started up the sidewalk.

I held the base of the pole between my feet positioned on the wheelchair. Its five small wheels squeeked under the weight of the two pumps, IV bags and oxygen tank, especially as we traversed over the sidewalk cracks, bricks, and aggregate payment. The incline leading up to an intersection at the Dayani Center presented additional problems, as Beverly struggled to push the wheelchair. We were an odd sight...a tiny Southern lady attempting to push a heavy wheelchair, occupied by a tall male tethered to oxygen and pumps. We were exhausted as I attempted to walk across the street and up the curb to the doorway. Beverly waited until the session was finished, and we completed the round trip to the hospital.

Beverly is representative of most employees associated with the transplant program at Vanderbilt...caring, professional, and empathetic to our fears, hopes and needs. She has always been supportive, available and helpful. After a transplant, the coordinator serves as the primary conduit between the patient and the medical staff concerning changes in medications, physical status, and business affairs.

Beverly was especially proud of her son. She said that her son had once told her, "Mommy, I love you so much that the wind would blow all of the trees down!" After being associated with Beverly before, during, and after the transplant, I can understand his deep affection for his mother.

♡ First False Alarm

Several days after qualifying on Vanderbilt's list, I was lying in bed watching the late edition of the news. Barb had returned to Zanesville to spend a few days with David, and to attend to some business. It was early morning when the telephone began to ring. I answered. It was Dr. Eastburn.

He said there was a possibility of an available heart, and I should be thinking about a transplant. I asked if I there was a high probability, and if I should call Barb. He said he thought that would be a good idea. Barb was 450 miles away. Barb immediately called our friend Bob England.

♡ Bob and Anne England

We met Bob and Anne while attending St. John Lutheran Church in Zanesville. Bob was an optometrist in town.

Bob and Anne have three children: Kirk, a student in Fremont, Ohio; Keith, serving our country in the U.S. Army; and Kristen, a beautiful blond student at Ohio State University.

Bob and Anne were very active in many organizations in town, and we had served on several committees together...Church Council and Goodwill Industries. We always enjoyed being with Anne and Bob. I had always envied Bob since he always appeared to be well organized and in control.

Both were also very talented, and had varied interests in music and choral arrangements. Best of all, they were caring individuals who always were there to help.

When I experienced the massive heart attack in 1988, I was able to drive to the church looking for Barb. It was Anne, also volunteering that afternoon, who first saw me in a fetal position on the floor. Her coolness under extreme stressful conditions enabled an ambulance to be summoned quickly.

Bob and Anne loved to fly, and maintained a twin engined Navajo at the Parr airport north of town. On several occasions, Anne would call Barb and I, and ask about our plans for dinner. We ended up at Latrobe, Pennsylvania one Sunday, and Put-in-Bay in Lake Erie on another occasion.

When I was interned at Ohio State, almost every day brought a card from Anne and Bob. They also prepared chili and sent me a new yellow power tie. I called Anne AMBE..<u>A</u>nne <u>M</u>arie <u>B</u>aker <u>E</u>ngland. We called Bob "Sky King" because he loved to fly the airplane.

Shortly after I had been approved for the transplant list at Vanderbilt, Dr. Ted Eastburn called and told me there was a possible heart that could be used for a transplant. Barb had returned to Zanesville for a few days, and I quickly called her. It was late at night.

Barb immediately phoned Bob, and told him of the call. He had previously volunteered his time and resources in our quest for a miracle. He called the weather bureau, the airport at Zanesville, and left a message on his office answering machine that he would not be in that morning. He called Barb back, and had her and David meet him at the airport before dawn. The low cloud cover did not prevent an obstacle as the beige plane began its climb to the Music City.

After the transplant, Bob and Anne attended a convention in San Francisco. They arrived just in time to experience the big earthquake that took place in the week following the transplant.

Barb was attempting to commute to Zanesville during the stay at Vanderbilt, and many of our friends that we had known when we had lived near Nashville maintained a steady vigil.

♡ Peggy Buchanan

We had met Peggy when we had lived in Franklin, Tennessee, a small town located near Nashville, and close to Spring Hill, site of the mammoth General Motors Saturn manufacturing plant.

Our families attended the Lutheran Church of St. Andrew, in Franklin during the late 70's. Our children were approximately the same age. Gary and Peggy Buchanan had three children: Mark, Jenny and Jason.

When we left Tennessee, Gary and Peggy went through a painful divorce, which hurt us because we thought so much of them and their family. For several years after the divorce, our contact was sporadic, with occasional phone calls.

Peggy is a petite and intelligent lady, who obtained a Masters degree, and works for the court system in Williamson County dealing with troubled teens. She is dedicated to her work, and very successful.

When I went to Vanderbilt for the transplant, Peggy threw her full resources into making the venture as painless as possible. She opened her home to Barb and our family, and maintained a loyal vigil at Vanderbilt when Barb returned to Zanesville.

Her visits and phone calls were frequent and supportive. At one time, I had expressed my disappointment that I did not have access to a stationary bicycle in the room. Several days later, Peggy visited me and brought screw drivers, crescent wrenches and an assortment of nuts, bolts and screws. She had mentioned my concern with some other friends, and they had all chipped in and bought a stationary bike to use in the room. Neither of us was mechanically inclined, but within hours the bicycle took form.

It was a great morale booster, as well as a physical rehabilitation device. I still try to ride the bike at least several evenings per week, and always remember the evening that Peggy and I spent sitting on the floor of the room assembling the vehicle.

I call Peggy whenever I return to Vanderbilt for the biopsies. She remains a loyal and loving friend to our family. I'll always remember her unflinching support during a traumatic period of our lives.

We continued to receive spiritual support from our former pastor in Tennessee, Eric Pearson. Pastor Pearson made the trek from Brentwood, a southern suburb of Nashville, many times each week. He was in the room when we were notified that a possible heart was available (a false alarm) and was with us when the nurses came for the operation.

♡ Pastor Eric Pearson

After we had moved to Franklin in 1977, we searched for a Lutheran Church near Nashville. We soon found out that Lutherans were a minority in the South. We finally contacted Eric Pearson, the Pastor of the Lutheran Church of St. Andrew.

The first week, we missed church because we could not find the building. Services were being held in the basement community room of a local bank. Each week, all the hymnals, collection plates, crosses, and organ were carried into the building, and removed after the service. Later, we moved to the country, sharing a building with a Methodist congregation, and finally raised enough money to construct a building in 1981. The congregation has grown by leaps and bounds, partially due to the construction of the General Motors Saturn plant in Spring Hill, Tennessee. Many "Damm Yankees" have moved to Tennessee to staff the new facility.

The growth is a tribute to Eric Pearson. He located to the South from Syracuse, New York with his wife Connie and daughter Alice. His son Tim, now an avid musician, was born after he arrived in Nashville.

Pastor Eric went door to door, recruiting Lutherans, and established St. Andrew in 1975. Shortly after Tim's birth, it was discovered that he had a severe heart problem, that required several operations. Pastor Pearson commented that being near Vanderbilt, with the expertise available for coronary problems was very fortuitous for his family. He is a man of deep conviction.

Barb and I came to love Pastor Pearson, not only as our spiritual leader, but also as a person. If God would have given me two brothers, Pastor Eric would have been a good brother. He was a frequent visitor to my room at Vanderbilt, coming almost every day. I remarked that we were no longer members of his congregation, yet his devotion was unending. He was also present when I was moved to the operating room for the transplant, and comforted Barb and I immediately before, and after the operation. I've never met a more compassionate, gentle, caring individual.

♡ Before the Operation

Several weeks after entering Vanderbilt, I was moved to a section of the hospital called the Cooperative Care unit. I had requested the transfer because I continued to be very concerned with the spiraling costs while waiting for the transplant. Thanks to Dr. Eastburn, I was able to be relocated, despite the fact that I continued to be connected to two IV pumps.

The facilities at the Cooperative Care unit were well suited for those patients needing minimal continuous nursing care. It was located in a round building, and the rooms were in a circle surrounding a central monitoring station. Each of the rooms was quite large, and included a couch, which folded into a bed, a desk and chairs. It seemed a lot like home after being in a cramped room for over six months. The unit was manned by several nurses and a monitor attendant. A small room near the station housed a microwave oven, a refrigerator and a pantry with soups, crackers, and other snacks. The atmosphere was totally professional, although much less formal than the other units.

Barbara continued to commute each week from Zanesville, a distance of about 450 miles. She would leave work at 2 o'clock on Friday, drive to Nashville, arriving about 11 o'clock. We would spend Saturday reading, resting, or watching television, and she would return to Zanesville on Sunday. The frantic pace that she set was Herculean.

One weekend, she managed to adjust her schedule, so that she could spend some extra time in Nashville. We felt it was a real treat, since we could spend a lot more time together. It was a beautiful Autumn afternoon in Nashville, and we decided to try to maneuver the poles and pumps outside, to sit on the patio of the building.

Workmen were raking leaves, and various small groups of students and teachers were strolling about the well manicured grounds. Barb and I pulled and pushed the IV pumps and oxygen across the lobby of the building and the pebbled patio to a small table. She spotted an additional chair across the patio, and brought it to the table. We began to talk.

We had been through a lot...almost seven months of various hospitals, now finding ourselves almost 450 miles away from our home in Ohio. We missed our family...we missed our home, and our friends and animals.

We wondered if God was telling us that we were not destined to have a transplant, and that we should go home to complete my life on Earth. I was worried about the strain that my illness had placed on my family, and the unseemingly endless procession of doctors, medical bills and worry. What was God's wish? I was willing to accept anything that He wanted.

We were discouraged. I knew what my fate was, if I went home to Zanesville and exited the program. Vanderbilt was my only hope for a transplant, and God had brought us a long way to be in Nashville. I also knew that our energies had diminished, and our quality of life in Ohio would be easier mentally.

We looked at each other. "Honey I'm ready to call it quits. I want to go home this weekend" I said to Barb.

Barb said "No, not now. Let's **Wait until Tuesday** when I have to return to Zanesville before we make that decision."

We didn't know it at that moment, but God knew that we would not have to make that decision.

♡ Yvonne Burton

We met Yvonne Burton when we lived in Franklin in the late 1970's. She, her sons Matt and Daniel, and husband Barry were next door neighbors.

Yvonne was a true southern belle... born, raised and educated near Nashville. She was a gentle, quiet and intelligent woman, a great mother and a caring person. Her small stature obscured her athletic ability. We frequently spotted her mowing the grass or attempting to complete projects at her house.

She was much handier than her husband Barry, a former all Southeast Conference football player at Vanderbilt, who played in the last College All-Star game in 1976. He was drafted by the Pittsburgh Steelers in the National Football League, was cut and played a season in Canada. We frequently played basketball in my driveway. Barry would overpower me, since he was considerably larger and stronger. I did manage to ask him if he had always worn his helmet when he played football, since he was often out of control.

The Burtons occasionally locked themselves out of their home, and would summon me for help. I would remove a storm window for Matt or

Daniel to craw through, and they would run to the front door and unlock the door. On other occasions, I would fix the window panes through which the boys had thrown pool balls. Yvonne did not know it at the time, but I learned many of my handyman skills at her home.

We moved in 1981, and kept correspondence through occasional calls, or notes at Christmas. When I was attempting to qualify for the transplant list at Vanderbilt, Yvonne opened her home to Barbara and our family. In addition, she and Daniel would trek to Vanderbilt and visit me during the week. Her visits were always appreciated, since she brought a great deal of grace and serenity to our lives. Yvonne was typical of the many wonderful friends that we have made in our lifetimes.

♡ Gary Buchanan

Gary Buchanan and I became friends when our family lived in Tennessee from 1977 to 1981. We both attended the Lutheran Church of St. Andrew in Franklin, a small town about 25 miles south of Nashville. We also had children about the same age. His wife, Peggy, and Barb were also very close friends.

We lost track of each other for about 7 years when he and Peggy decided to terminate their marriage. We continued to correspond with Peggy, and traded school pictures of our kids during Christmas seasons.

Gary remarried, and I was disappointed that we hadn't maintained our friendship. I think Gary felt awkward that his marriage had failed, and we had remained close to Peggy. Whenever we talked with Peggy, we always asked how Gary was doing. We heard that he had remarried, and was very happy. That made us happy.

When I went to Vanderbilt, Peggy would visit me, and mentioned that Gary wanted to see me. I was thrilled that he would come to Vanderbilt. Several days later, a familiar face appeared in the doorway...it was my friend Gary.

Within a few minutes, it was like we had never been apart. That's the wonderful thing about some friendships...contrary to popular beliefs, absence often makes the heart grow fonder. Gary came to visit many times. Sometimes he would bring books or magazines, or sneak a ham sandwich from the cafeteria at Vanderbilt. He even brought a 1990

Marilyn Monroe calendar in September. At that time, I told him that it was doubtful that I would ever use it, but he kept encouraging me.

Sometimes I stay with Gary and Rejeanna, his new wife, when I journey to Zanesville for testing. He frequently calls between visits, to make sure everything is going o.k., and discuss sports or business. We also laugh a lot.

Our relationship is special because we've been through traumatic experiences, including heart attacks, transplants, and a divorce, as well as a long period of not seeing each other, but our friendship has endured.

♡ Sunday

Sunday was an uneventful day. Barb and I spent most of the day working on several paint by number kits. We also worked on a picture album of a trip that David, my Mom and Dad, and I took to Alaska two years before. We were also viewing several professional football games that were on the television.

Since Barb did not have a great affinity, or understanding of football, we were both waiting for the evening news and programming. 60 Minutes had always been one of our favorite shows, and we were anticipating its showing. The football game seemed to be dragging on and on...I couldn't wait for it to end.

At about 8 o'clock, I began to experience difficulty with an IV that began to back up. A solution of blood and medication began to leak onto the hospital gown and bedding, and I rang for Emily, the weekend nurse. Emily quickly appeared within 30 seconds, and agreed that the tubing needed to be changed. We shut off the pumps, and Emily quickly and efficiently began the arduous task of changing the tubing. It was quite an ordeal...the bedding had become crimson red very quickly.

During the conversion, Donna, the unit secretary, called for Emily to tell her that Dr. Frist wanted to speak with her. Emily looked at me, and shouted to Donna that she would call Dr. Frist back in a few minutes. The conversion was completed, and Emily left to call Dr. Frist. I looked over at Barb, who was sitting on the couch. My heart began to race, and I was almost overcome by a strange feeling. I felt that God's hand was near me.

Emily came back into the room. She was very composed, but excited.

Dr. Frist had wanted to know my exact medical condition, since there was a possibility that a heart was going to be available for transplant by morning. In a few minutes, Dr. Frist called me with the information. It was the first time that I had spoken to him, since he had been on a sabbatical since I had entered the hospital.

Dr. Frist apologized that he had not spoken with me sooner. He had returned earlier during the week, and had attempted to catch up on some of his paperwork. He said that a heart was available in the Nashville area that appeared to be suitable for transplant, but there were several issues which needed to be resolved prior to a final decision. He requested that Emily call him in about two hours for additional information, and to relax until we spoke again.

The next two hours were about as long as any that any of us will ever spend. All of the emotions in our lifetimes are experienced. We think of our families and friends, and our hopes and fears. We ponder our faith. I thought of the donor and their family, and the conflict and fear and courage that they were experiencing. I had been through false starts before...this was not to be a false start.

When the two hours were up, Emily called Dr. Frist. She came back into the room...the news indicated that the heart was in good condition, and the transplant procedures were going to the next step. I was extremely nervous, but confident. The long months in the hospital, the endless tests and waiting were suddenly paying off. I was confident that our Lord would be with me, just as He had always been.

Barb and I tried to act normal during the final wait. We called my Mom and Dad, as well as my brother. We called our friend Peggy Buchanan and our pastor at the Lutheran Church of St. Andrew in Franklin, Pastor Eric Pearson. Peggy and Pastor Pearson were eager to come to the hospital to lend support.

I took a final shower, and Barb took a shower and washed her hair. The hours drug on as the wait continued. Another phone call confirmed that everything was going as scheduled. The protocol continued as more tests were conducted. Finally, Pastor Pearson and Peggy appeared shortly before I was taken down to the operating room. We had a prayer and a wonderful discussion. A nurse appeared in the room...it was time to go.

I said good-bye to Peggy and Pastor Pearson, and the nurse wheeled the gurney into the hall and through the tunnels leading through the hospital complex. Barb held my hand as we neared the surgical unit. We stopped at the door, as Barb was not permitted any further. We kissed, and I told her that I loved her. The doors opened and I saw Barb disappear as they slowly closed.

The room was cool, and I asked for an additional blanket. Several technicians were hooking up instruments, as the room was jammed with gauges, pumps and all types of sophisticated machines. One of the male technicians took my hand and inserted a catheter..he said it would automatically take my blood pressure. He asked if I needed anything, and I requested something to dampen my nervousness. I told him to do whatever he wanted to do...that he was the boss. It was the last thing that I remember saying until I woke up the following afternoon with a new heart.

♡ Dr. William H. Frist

Dr. William Frist performed my transplant on October 9, 1989.

I first spoke with him on October 8, when he called to let me know there was a possibility of a transplant. He had been on a sabbatical from the moment that I entered Vanderbilt until the Sunday evening when he called. He apologized that our first contact was such a serious matter.

Dr. Frist was the son of a prominent Nashville family. His father, as well as several brothers, had been prominent in the Nashville medical community. His dad (Dr. Thomas Frist), in fact, was one of the primary founders of Hospital Corporation of America, one of the largest, and most successful corporations in the United States.

Dr. Frist was a graduate of Princeton University, and graduated from the Harvard Medical School. He was a surgical resident at Massachusetts General Hospital and served under Dr. Norman Shumway, the brilliant pioneer of heart transplant technology at Stanford University. His position at Stanford as a senior fellow in transplantation, when the program was the country's leading transplant center, provided him with an excellent opportunity to develop his considerable administrative and medical skills..

Dr. Shumway is considered by most experts as the foremost authority on transplants, and probably would have performed the first heart transplant, had Christian Barnard of South Africa not jumped the gun in 1967. His many procedures have become the basis of many successful programs in the world. Dr. Frist gives much of the credit for his success to Dr. Shumway.

Dr. Frist had returned to Nashville to develop the transplant program at Vanderbilt. Prior to his arrival, the success of the program had been marginal. He quickly immersed himself in the program, and through dedication and hard work developed it to one of the most successful in the world.

I have been impressed by Dr. Frist's demeanor. He is a quintessent southern gentleman, with a sincere interest in his patients. He is a devoted father of three sons and a loving son, brother and husband. He always greets me when I see him, an impressive feat to me, since my visits are infrequent and he meets hundreds of new faces each month.

Dr. Frist wrote <u>Transplant: A Heart Surgeon's Account of the Life-and-Death Dramas of the New Medicine.</u> I refer to his book frequently, and advise many people to read it. He also provides an organ donor card in the book jacket of his publication. He is a tireless speaker and advocate of transplants, and has appeared on the Today show, as well as countless panels to promote the gift of life.

I am alive today in large part to Dr. Frist. He and his staff did not have to accept me into the Vanderbilt program. His acceptance was almost the last option that remained for me when I was on death's doorstep.

I often have the opportunity of discussing the miracle of transplants. I recommend prospective recipients to consider Vanderbilt, even if its location is not convenient to some patients. Transplantation is a long term proposal, and the inconvenience of commuting for biopsies is a small price to pay to become part of a successful program.

Despite his many successes, Dr. Frist has not lost the common touch... the ability to make a person feel important regardless of their status in life. He is a humanitarian, as well as one of the most brilliant men that I've ever met.

When I became conscious after the operation, I heard Barb and my brother Joe talking to me.

♡ Joe- Transplant

I woke up from the operation when I heard Barb speaking to me. Joe had flown to Nashville from New England, where we had contacted him on his vacation. He had arrived as I was in the operating room, and maintained a vigil with Pastor Pearson, Peggy Buchanan and Barb. Joe and Barb entered the room and saw the numerous pumps and tubes leading into my body. My appearance was frightening, since during the operation, my body had gained over 20 pounds due to the infusion of countless fluids. My face and head were the most distorted, as it took the form of a pumpkin. Barb and Joe were not certain at first that it was their brother and husband lying on the table.

I could not talk, since the breathing apparatus had been inserted in my throat. When I heard them speaking to me, I started to make motions on my chest. They were not sure, at first what I was attempting to do, and thought I was asking for water. They soon realized I was spelling out a message. They started to sound out the letters...G...O...D...I...S...W...I...T...H...M...E. The letters were put together...<u>God is with me</u>. What a miracle! I was experiencing something that only a few thousand people had ever experienced...the heart of a stranger beating in my chest.

Several days later, Joe and David went shopping. They went to some malls surrounding Nashville, and returned with a blue t-shirt with a red heart and white lettering. The shirt's lettering said "I had a change of heart at Vanderbilt on October 9, 1989".

Joe presented the t-shirt to me when I was able to appreciate it. I wore it for our family Christmas card picture, as well as the picture on the front page of the TIMES RECORDER with Andy Mast, my little friend when we went to McDonald's for lunch several weeks later.

♡ San Francisco Earthquake

Eight days after the transplant, on October 17, 1989, I had ridden the stationary bike for several miles, and was preparing to watch the third game of the World Series between the Oakland Athletics and the San Francisco Giants.

Suddenly, as Al Michaels was doing his pregame analysis, a tremor measuring 7.1 on the Richter Scale suddenly rocked northern California. The quake was the fifth strongest in our history, and resulted in the deaths of more than 60 people and the damage of 100,000 houses. Congress later passed an aid package of $ 4.15 billion, while state officials pegged the damage at $ 5.6 billion.

I watched the drama unfolding on the screen, and walked out into the hall to tell others of the tragedy. Several people looked at me with disbelief, as I told them of the damage.

In our lifetimes, we often remember where we were, and what we were doing, when certain significant events occurred in our history. I'm sure we remember where we were when President Kennedy was assassinated in 1963, and when men first landed on the moon. I'll never forget where I was when the earthquake of 1989 rocked San Francisco. I was getting used to my new heart in Nashville, Tennessee. Some good friends of our family will also remember. Bob England, our friend from Zanesville, who had flown Barbara to Nashville, and his wife Anne were at Fisherman's Wharf when the ground rolled.

♡ Release from Vanderbilt

On Friday, eleven days after the transplant, I was released from Vanderbilt to stay at the Medical Arts Motel, located next to a parking lot at the hospital.

Barb and my Mom and Dad assisted the nurse in moving my belongings. It was a great feeling. The final wires connected to my heart had been removed the night before, the first time in over seven months that I was free of tubes or wires. The ride in the wheel chair went quickly, and we ascended the elevator to the seventh floor.

It was lunch time, and Dad asked me what I wanted to eat more than anything. The motel's location was convenient to all types of cuisine. We finally decided on Chinese food, without the salt or soy sauce. In addition, there was a Chinese restaurant located on the ground floor of the building.

Later that afternoon, one of my closest friends from my days at Aladdin, Ed Glaser, came to visit with champagne to celebrate. It was a special time for us. Ed had been one of my closest supporters during my stay at Vanderbilt. We had been friends for almost nine years and had spent several years at Aladdin. Ed had, in fact, been an employee at Aladdin for over 40 years, having joined the company when it had moved from Chicago in 1949. He was brilliant with numbers and loved sports, especially Kentucky basketball and all Vanderbilt sports.

Mom and Dad left for Maryland the next morning. They had spent about 10 days in Nashville, visiting several times each day, and returning to the Medical Arts Motel for quick naps. Their visits consisted of donning the blue masks, washing their hands and maintaining a vigil in my room.

They had spent a lot of time with me in the preceding two years. The heart attack in 1987 had brought them to Zanesville's Good Samaritan Medical Center, and the awful heart attack in 1988 brought them to Bethesda Hospital, and later to Ohio State University Hospital when my condition was grave. They also came to Bethesda Hospital in August when Beth was married in the chapel. Their return to Maryland on Saturday was a milestone for them...the culmination of a long struggle.

On Sunday, Barb and I decided to ride around Nashville, and to survey the changes in the city since we had moved in 1981. I walked part of the way to the car, but the incline of the sidewalk left me quickly gasping for air. I sat on a bench while Barb found the car. We began to drive around the "Athens of the South", one of the most beautiful cities in the United States. I watched the beautiful foliage of the trees as we proceeded toward Franklin, our old home. It was still early in the morning, and we considered going to our old church, the Lutheran Church of St. Andrew. We finally decided against church, since we were afraid of the crowd, and the possibility of catching a cold.

We spent a few minutes in Walmart, looking for a pair of inexpensive athletic shoes. There was a physical therapy session scheduled for the following afternoon, and all of my athletic shoes were still in Zanesville. We located a pair, and I wore them the rest of the afternoon.

We rode out to our old home in Green Valley. A lot had changed. The many small shrubs and trees that we had planted 10 years before were now large and beautiful. The lawn was lush and green, the result of many years of careful cultivation and care. The small bridge that I had made to permit David and his friend Matt Burton to enter the back part of the property was still in place, albeit with numerous repairs. We visited with one of our former neighbors, Sandy DuAime and her husband.

We ate lunch, and returned to the room. We had accomplished much on this beautiful, sunny afternoon. The memories of our past, when our lives were much simpler, had been rekindled. I envisioned David learning to ride his green bicycle without the training wheels, Beth's ballet classes and their small wading pool that instantly collapsed after they began to splash around.

When we arrived at the room, there was a message stuck in the door. Two friends from Virginia, Larry and Julie Reiniger had driven through the night from Norfolk to visit! When we weren't in the room, they went to the movies, and called when the movie was over. We had a wonderful visit, and they left at dusk for the long trip back to Virginia. We felt so good that they had taken two days from their busy schedule to visit us in Nashville.

On Monday, Barb and I drove to a pancake house for breakfast, and back to the motel prior to the physical therapy session. When we arrived at the Dayani Center for the workout with Jay Groves, he took my blood pressure. It was extremely low. He cautioned against a workout, and called the transplant center to inform them of the problem.

Barb and I walked to the car, and decided to tour Nashville. We spent most of the afternoon casually driving around the city. We also spent time at a Kroger store stocking up with provisions. The only moment when I felt strange was when we stopped for gasoline at a self-serve station. The fumes from the nozzle left me somewhat dizzy for a few minutes.

When we arrived at the motel there were several urgent messages from Bev Walker to call immediately. I called...Beverly was frantic. Beverly had evidently done everything possible to locate Barb and I, since one of the first signs of rejection is low blood pressure. I was ordered to come to the hospital immediately in a wheelchair.

I was given an echogram and EKG. Beverly suggested that I be admitted to the hospital. I objected strenuously, since I had been a patient so long that I was not going to be admitted easily. The few days away from the pumps, the tubing and the wires had spoiled me. I had visions of another extensive hospital stay. The tests came back negative, meaning no rejection. I was relieved that I would not be admitted. Barb and I returned to the efficiency apartment at the Medical Arts Building, where we had a quiet and uneventful evening. The shadow of rejection would continue to be a major concern throughout the next several months.

The trip from Nashville enabled me to have lunch with Andy Mast, one of my most loyal supporters.

♡ Andy Mast

One of my best and most loyal friends during the illness was Andy Mast. Andy was the five year old son of some friends at church...Pat and John Mast.

At the inception of the illness, Pat had told Andy about her friend, and Andy volunteered to send a few of his drawings to me at the hospital.

During the next year, Andy's drawings came on a regular basis, together with pictures of him and his little sister Abby. Andy took a special interest in me, and I told him that I was going to get well, and would take him to McDonald's for a Happy Meal when I was better. I so much wanted to keep the promise to Andy. He was loyal and loving, and would frequently ask his Mom when I was going to have the new heart. I understand that I was frequently mentioned in his prayers at night. We all should be so lucky to have a friend like Andy.

Several weeks after the operation, we returned to Zanesville for the weekend. I called Pat, and she arranged for Andy and I to meet for lunch at McDonald's. The photographer from the local newspaper captured the event, and it appeared on the first page of the local newspaper. The picture has remained on the Mast's refrigerator since it was published. It was a golden moment for me...A chance to return, in small part, so much that the little towheaded boy had given to me.

I still see my friend Andy frequently at church. I think he will always be as kind, considerate and loving as he was when he was helping me to survive. We can all learn important lessons of loyalty from his example.

♡ The Wait

Time moves slowly when you are waiting for a transplant, and the seven months spent waiting in the various hospitals saw many significant news stories.

One of our country's most publicized ecological mishaps, the grounding of the Exxon Valdez on March 24, came one week after I was admitted to Ohio State University Hospitals, spilling 10,000,000 gallons of crude oil on the pristine waters of Prince William Sound. I had remembered our vacation in 1987, when I, my Mom and Dad, and David had visited Alaska, and we had spent a Summer afternoon in Valdez. What a beautiful sight, with majestic, snow covered mountains, waterfalls and deep fjords. We had gone to the waterfront, and inspected the rich catch of salmon.

I felt sadness, as the pictures of dead and injured animals were flashed on tv screens across the country.

From the hospital bed in Columbus, I watched history unfold in China, as the students rebelled for more freedom. The subsequent slaughter in Tiananmen Square on June 3 and 4 brought additional sadness, as thousands of demonstrators were killed.

From the Bethesda Hospital CCU, I watched as Pete Rose, the manager of Cincinnati's beloved Reds, continued to declare his innocence on gambling charges.

After I arrived at Vanderbilt in September, I watched Hurricane Hugo advance to the South Carolina coast, and smash into Charleston with intense fury on September 21 and 22.

Finally, on October 17, the San Francisco earthquake before the third game of the World Series, between the Athletics and the Giants rocked the West Coast. It also happened when I was in a hospital.

I had watched the world changing from a bed. I vowed I would do everything in my power to help others waiting for transplants in the future, by publicizing the critical need for organ donors. Others would die waiting. I was lucky. God had spared me, for whatever reason. One of my other friends had not been as lucky.

♡ Roger Goddard

I first met Roger Goddard while waiting for a heart transplant at Ohio State University Hospital.

Roger was 45 years old, and a real live wire...very gregarious and outspoken, with a quick wit and outstanding business mind. He had been a manager at a security company that developed and installed security devices. Roger's forte was in the sales and marketing end of the business.

Roger attempted to qualify for the list at Ohio State, only to be rejected due to lung pressure complications. He was advised to try for inclusion on the list at Pittsburgh, where heart/lung transplants were more common.

While Roger was waiting for additional tests, he was interviewed by a reporter from the local newspaper in Newark. He expressed quite eloquently how it felt to be a possible organ recipient, and much of the emotional strain required to endure the long evaluation process. During the interview, he commented that the person that he really felt sorry for was his friend in Zanesville who was over 6 feet tall, and who had spent so much time waiting.

He commented he was particularly interested in hearing of trauma cases in, or near Columbus, since his friend was a priority transplant candidate. Roger had a deep commitment to his friends.

Roger visited me when I was at Bethesda Hospital, waiting for the transfer to Vanderbilt. Although tests showed that he was critically ill, Roger had put additional testing into limbo because he felt so good. He often commented he was the healthiest looking sick person he had ever seen. He enjoyed the majority of 1989 with his family.

Roger was concerned about the cost of the operation. Whereas the expense of heart transplants were generally covered by Medicare payments, combination heart/lung operations were considered experimental, and not covered.

After my successful operation at Vanderbilt, I called Roger during one of our visits back to Zanesville, approximately one week prior to Thanksgiving. I encouraged Roger to consider the program at Vanderbilt. He was encouraged by the good news...any good news for friends was felt by Roger. He shared in the joys and sorrows of friends because he was a good friend.

We agreed to meet for lunch, prior to Christmas, at a small ice cream shop in Zanesville during one of our visits home. I eagerly anticipated our meeting, since I had discussed Roger's condition with Dr. Frist, who seemed interested in evaluating Roger for inclusion on the list.

Barb and I discussed Roger and his condition as we returned from

Nashville. It was time to convince Roger that his future could be bright with a transplant.

Several days later, Barb and David went Christmas shopping at the mall, and I noticed the mail truck pulling away from the box. I trudged to the mail receptacle, emptied the contents, and returned to the house. Once inside the house, I quickly separated the pile into bills, magazines, advertisements, and Christmas cards. I began to open the Christmas cards, and inadvertently opened one addressed to Barb, with a return address of Newark. I thought the card would be from Roger, his wife Pat, and family.

There was not a card, but a letter from Pat. The letter, addressed to Barb, stated that Roger had died on December 2, and Pat was not sure how to tell me. I read the letter again and again. I cried. I could not believe that another good friend had died. A man with a loving wife and family was another casualty due to a lack of donor organs.

Roger was a good and brave man. He cared about his family, his community and his country. Now he was gone. I felt a terrible loss.

♡ Christmas, 1989

The first few months after a transplant are filled with anxiety, as you and your body become accustomed to the transplanted heart. You experience an emotional roller coaster as you remember how close you came to death, and realize that infection and rejection will always be close at hand.

Christmas was a wonderful day at our house, as we celebrated Jesus' birth, and had the opportunity of having many phone calls from our families and friends.

I had a biopsy scheduled at Vanderbilt for December 27, and we had asked one of David's friends, Jim Miller, if he would like to go to Nashville with us. Jim was a bright young man, an avid crosscountry runner and an honor student at Zanesville High School. Jim was one of the nicest young people that I've ever met.

The drive to Nashville was uneventful, although Jim became excited as we came near the city. It was his first trip to the "Athens of the South", and his Mom, grandma, and younger brother (Scotty) had asked him to buy souvenirs during his visit.

The biopsy was uneventful the next morning, and we went on a tour of Nashville in the afternoon, spending time at the Cumberland Museum. In addition, we went to a hockey game featuring the Nashville Knights. It was Jim's first ice hockey game, and we were all excited by the action.

The following day, we went on another tour around Nashville and drove by the homes of Ray Stevens, Minnie Pearl, Tammy Wynette and Webb Pierce. When the activity for the evening was being voted upon, both Jim and David opted for another hockey game. Prior to the game, we went to downtown Nashville and walked to the Hyatt Regency, one of the tallest structures in Nashville, and one with a revolving restaurant on the top. We thought it would be unique for Jim and David if we could have lunch in the restaurant, and to obtain a panoramic view of the city.

The weather was chilly and damp, and I noticed that I was having a great deal of difficulty in navigating slopes and steps. I would have to rest after several steps, but attributed the problem to the humidity, and just being tired. I was determined that our trip was going to be enjoyable for our family. Jim, Barb and David rode the glass elevators on the atrium of the Hyatt Regency after we were disappointed in finding the restaurant closed for repairs. The hockey game that evening proved to be exciting, as the Knights overcame an early deficit to snatch victory from the jaws of defeat.

♡ New Year's- 1990

The biopsy at Vanderbilt had not uncovered anything alarming, and another was not scheduled for two weeks. We did agree that blood work would be done at Bethesda Hospital, with the results telecopied to Vanderbilt for evaluation. In addition, a vial of blood would be sent to Vanderbilt for a cyclosporine level evaluation on a weekly basis.

I was now driving alone, and I went to Bethesda's emergency room on the morning of December 31 to register for the blood work. There had evidently been a busy morning, as all of the parking spots were taken. I parked at the bottom of a slope and began to walk up the incline. I was laboring like I had prior to the operation, but felt that I had not properly warmed up and the dampness was compounding the problem.

I stopped two or three times to rest...I couldn't believe that I couldn't run up the incline, much less walk up. I eventually made it to the lab, had the blood drawn, and mailed the samples to Nashville.

My condition improved that day, and we had some close friends over to our home that evening to celebrate the coming of the new year. I did however, feel tired, and was looking forward to New Year's Day and the many football bowl games, especially the Orange Bowl between Colorado and Notre Dame.

I woke up on New Year's Day with absolutely no energy, and a slight fever. The weather was cold, damp and depressing. Barb told me to stay in bed...it sounded like a good idea to me. Around noon, I decided to take a shower. I stumbled into the bathroom, turned on the faucets, and prepared to take a warm shower. I hesitated to climb into the shower. I realized that I didn't feel strong enough to stand up long enough to take the shower. I decided to take a bath, and flipped the plug, and waited for the tub to fill. After a few minutes, I turned the water off, and climbed in the tub.

The water felt very relaxing, but as I found out later, a hot bath was not good for me, as it caused a severe fluctuation with my blood pressure. I tried to get out of the tub, but kept slipping. I finally called out for Barb, who came running. We eventually were successful, and made it to the bedroom.

I became more concerned when my temperature did not recede, and breathing became more difficult. Barb called Dr. Jones, my Zanesville cardiologist for advise. He was out of town. She then called Vanderbilt, who advised us to come in immediately. Since the weather was so poor and it was a holiday, with limited scheduled flights, our only option was to drive the 450 miles to Nashville. The 9 hour drive under possible adverse weather conditions would be a harrowing experience.

Darkness was close at hand as we began our trip. Interstate 70 was slippery, and we were hoping that sufficient salt and cinders would prevent slippery conditions.

As we came to Columbus, darkness had permeated the day. We drove around the Columbus bypass, and headed south on Interstate 71 toward Cincinnati. The weather was cold and damp. Barb asked if I was hungry.

I was, but suggested that we try to get closer to our destination, just in case I was to get sick. I was having problems breathing, but didn't want to alarm Barb. The 100 miles between Columbus and Cincinnati were uneventful...Barb and I didn't talk too much, and I didn't want to distract her from concentrating on the drive.

We finally stopped about 75 miles south of Cincinnati, close to Louisville. We stopped for gas, and I climbed out of the car to fill the tank. The wind and cold were oppressive as I filled the tank. I was totally exhausted when I sat back in the seat. I knew that I was having a serious problem. I had been told to expect rejection, and that virtually everyone who had a transplant went through a period when the body's immune system attempted to reject the transplanted organ.

The transplant had been too easy. The biopsies had gone well, and reflected only minor rejection. The rehab period was progressing nicely, and the dormant muscles were becoming strong again. I had managed to escape most of the serious side effects that I had been expecting, and was looking forward to a long and productive life. As we approached Nashville, it was close to midnight. I wondered if I would ever be able to return home again. The breathing was becoming more strained, and I knew I was in serious trouble.

When we arrived at Vanderbilt, I became argumentative with the emergency room doctor. He wanted to draw new blood samples. I argued that I had results of tests taken that morning at Bethesda in Zanesville. I was concerned about the cost, and the declining benefits remaining on the insurance policy. He called Dr. Eastburn, who quickly resolved the conflict...the blood was drawn.

A complete battery of testing was performed...x-rays, blood gases and normal blood draws. I felt lousy...I had just enough strength to give the doctors and technicians a hard time. Somehow, I knew that I had come too far to give up. I was determined to fight to the end.

I was told to remove my clothing, and change into the hospital garb... the clothing which completely strips a patient of their dignity...the gown which reveals your rear end despite one's best efforts to maintain their modesty.

The next day, I heard the dreaded words...rejection and virus. These were the words that I had heard regarding my friend Jimmie Taylor's death after his transplant. Could it be that the same malady would prove to be my demise? My breathing was becoming more and more labored. I could muster only enough strength to move five steps to the bathroom, and would huff and puff when I came back to the bed.

I was ushered down to the cath lab for a biopsy and to another room for an echocardiogram and an EKG...the tests seemed endless, and I was not getting any better. Dr. Eastburn did say that I had a virus, and they were trying to isolate its location. About the same time, another transplant patient had been brought into the hospital, and was placed on a respirator. Dr. Eastburn seemed annoyed that the patient had not followed precautions, and was now in a life-and-death struggle.

The relationship became strained, as I became weary of the tests, the needles and the atmosphere of the hospital. I kept wondering why all the tests, all the blood draws, all the x-rays, the biopsies, the echocardiograms, the EKG the urine samples had not revealed where the problem was located. I finally said "Enough is enough. Review all of the tests and reach a conclusion, because I am not going to submit to additional expensive and painful testing."

Several hours later, another pair of doctors appeared in the doorway with a consent form. I told them that I wasn't going to submit to any more tests. Despite their best persuasive arguments, they left without my signature.

They had wanted to do another biopsy, this time of my lung. The access would be through my nose. The very thought completely frightened me. Barb and I looked at each other, and knew what really had to be done. A few minutes later, the supervisor of the doctors that I had just refused entered the room, and explained that they would do everything possible to minimize the discomfort of the test. I signed the form and waited for the test.

The test was not as bad as I had envisioned, as I daydreamed and did everything that I possibly could to keep my mind occupied. The test revealed that the virus had attacked my lungs, and was treated through a heavy regimen of antibiotics, many of which could be administered as an outpatient.

I spent ten more days in Nashville after I was released from the hospital. My Dad came down to Nashville to stay with me. I wanted Barb to come back to Zanesville to be with David, and also to be with our daughter Beth, who was expecting our first grandchild. Dad and I went to the hospital twice each day for the IV drugs required to clear up the virus. I had survived a major setback.

♡ Emotions

Post transplant activity brings an additional set of new worries and concerns, including the fear of rejection, and believing that additional "chances" will not be forthcoming. The recipient becomes aware of simple colds, aches (which could signal infection or rejection) and the periodic biopsies. Heavy medication can bring harm to other body organs which could eventually cause death.

You also have to completely evaluate life. I see friends dying from heart problems and ask...why them and not me?...why am I still alive?... How should I be spending my life?...should I be actively attempting to promote organ donations, or should I be taking life easy? The answers are not easy. I suppose that one day we will know the answer, but today we are not wise enough.

♡ Medications

Heavy amounts of medication are taken after the transplant to prevent the body's immune system from rejecting the transplanted organ. Since everyone is different, adjustments are required for the entire lifetime of the recipient. Generally, the amount of medication will be decreased as the time from the transplant increases, but will never be completely stopped.

The amount of required medication depends upon the closeness of the match, and the compatibility with the recipient. The age of the recipient, interestingly enough, sometimes determines the amount of medication. Generally, patients who are infants will require less medication, since the immune system has not had the opportunity of developing.

A person who does not take their medicine as prescribed runs an immediate high risk, and is considered non compliant. Non compliance is the third major cause of transplant failure. It is considered the most important function of a transplant recipient after their operation.

♡ Sandimmune (Cyclosporine)

The major antirejection drug taken after the operation is Sandimmune, manufactured by Sandoz Pharmaceuticals Corporation of Switzerland. Sandimmune was originally a liquid, taken with chocolate milk. It is now available in tablet form.

The discovery of Sandimmune, the "magic bullet", constituted a major breakthrough in transplant technology. Prior to its discovery, success rates for transplants were not high. It was discovered in 1972, the result of a scientist carrying a soil sample to the lab from his vacation. It was first used on humans in 1976.

In 1980, it was used on all types of transplants with good success. On liver transplants, for example, the success rate increased from 35 % to 60 %. Kidney transplants at Stanford University reflected an increased success rate from 63 % to 83 %. It received FDA approval in 1980.

The introduction of Sandimmune constituted a replacement or supplement to anti-rejection drugs then in use, without some of the major drawbacks of other drugs.

It acts specifically to inhibit the action of the helper T cells. Other immunossuppressant drugs suppress many kinds of cells, causing adverse effects, such as infection. Sandimmune does not decrease the function of bone marrow, responsible for the production of red blood cells.

There are side effects of all drugs, and Sandimmune is no exception. The most common side effects include kidney dysfunction, such as a decrease in output, fever, and swollen feet and hands, high blood pressure, headache and tremor. Other side effects include stomach discomfort, acne, cramps, diarrhea, liver toxicity, and burning or tingling sensations on the skin.

♡ Prednisone

Prednisone is a corticosteroid similar to a hormone produced naturally by the body, and is necessary to produce good health. It is taken with other medications to prevent rejection, and is taken as long as you have a transplanted organ.

It was one of the mainstay drugs used in the field of transplantation, but produced undesired side effects. Some of the side effects included mood changes, acne, stomach irritation, continuing infections, a "moon face", muscle cramps, muscle weakness, unusual tiredness and weight gain. Some patients also experienced severe headaches, indigestion, restlessness, an increase in appetite and nervousness.

Mood changes can occur very quickly. I often feel changes coming on where I feel great one minute, and suddenly feel depressed. The change can be minimized if you feel it coming, by changing the activity that you are doing, perhaps by turning on the television or exercising.

I think this is the reason why a team of psychiatrists examine you prior to acceptance in most programs, as you must be able to handle the emotional problem when it occurs after the transplant. You must also be careful that the disruption on your family is minimized.

The stomach irritation could lead to bleeding ulcers. You are normally required to take an antacid between meals, to reduce the probability of problems. The antacid is purchased over the counter.

Continuing infections are due to the suppression of the immune system. The body's immune system attacks foreign invaders such as viruses and colds. Unfortunately, the body does not recognize a good foreign body (a transplanted organ) from a bad foreign body (a virus), and will try to destroy anything foreign entering your system. Thus, the suppression of the immune system to allow acceptance of the transplant also allows unwanted virus germs to prosper in the body, increasing the probability of colds, etc.

The medication causes the patient's face to become rounded, like a chipmunk. I found this problem to be very noticeable, but an acceptable side effect. Some transplant patients, or their spouses, consider it to be a major problem since appearance can change markedly.

There have been cases where a patient ceases to take the medication because they can not accept the change of their appearance. As was mentioned before, a sure way to cause severe problems is to stop taking the prescribed medication.

There was also severe discomfort after the surgery with muscle cramps and soreness. The cramps were similar to charley-horses, and caused considerable pain. The cure was to take magnesium tablets (purchased over the counter) each morning. The cramps occurred in my hands and legs, and lasted up to 20 minutes.

The weight gain is caused by an increased appetite and fluid retention. The increased appetite is experienced by most patients, and in my case may have been caused, in part, by the severe craving of food prior to the operation. All foods taste extremely good, especially after you've lost 60 pounds prior to the surgery.

The fluid retention is treated by taking a diuretic each morning. It is not unusual to have a severe gain due to the fluid retention. When medication is taken, the fluid imbalance requires a potassium supplement, in order to maintain the electrolyte balance in the blood.

The muscle weakness requires an exercise regimen including walking, floor exercises or riding a stationary bicycle.

Prednisone also affects the functioning of the adrenal glands that produce adrenaline.

♡ Imuran

Imuran is another immunosuppressant used in conjunction with cyclosporine and prednisone. The side effects include an increased risk of infection, nausea, hair loss and decreased white blood cell count. There is also a possibility of liver dysfunction.

♡ Other Drugs

Many other drugs or supplements are required after the transplant. Most, however are reduced as the time from a transplant increases.

Today, I still take a baby aspirin each morning, together with an ACE inhibitor to treat high blood pressure. The inhibitor can cause dizziness, fever, joint pain or skin rash.

There is also a pill to prevent stomach ulcers, anti-fungal medication to fight thrush (a fungal infection of the mouth) as well as the antacid.

♡ Importance

Each of the subject drugs are required to assure the best chance of a successful transplant. There have been cases where patients have become depressed and did not take their medication as prescribed, causing immediate problems.

Patients must make a commitment to adhere to the schedules, and follow all orders as directed by the transplant personnel. The nurses at Vanderbilt would constantly have little quizzes regarding each drug, their dosage, purpose, the time that the doses are taken, their physical appearance, etc. When you leave the hospital, your care depends on how well you have learned the lessons.

The personnel at the hospital also review and discuss other facets of your care, including diet, exercise regimen prior to leaving for home. Patients are instructed when, and how to take blood pressure, temperature and pulse. Any signs of rejection are reported immediately to the transplant personnel.

♡ Cost

Transplantation is a very expensive process, and requires significant financial resources. The only means available to most prospective recipients are private insurance plans.

My insurance was provided by my employer, Cooper Industries, and administered through Aetna Insurance Company. The policy contained a lifetime maximum of $ 500,000. The heart transplant provision was in the guidelines of the plan, although many other policies consider the procedure to be experimental, and thus will not cover the cost.

The long wait for a donor heart in Ohio State University Hospital, Bethesda Hospital, and Vanderbilt University Medical Center liquidated over $ 300,000 of the lifetime allowance. The actual operation, medication, hospitalization in January 1990, and follow up liquidated the balance of the lifetime allowance.

The cost of the procedure could be significantly reduced if available organs could be increased, thus reducing the wait in a hospital. The miracle of modern medicine is a two-edged sword...we have the ability to diagnose terminal heart failure, and extend life through the administration of new drugs. The patients can anticipate an extended life only through a transplant. Until the operation, they must be maintained in a hospital, with costs approaching $ 1,500 per day. Potential recipients are identified earlier, thus increasing the length of waiting lists.

Unfortunately, approximately 1/3 of all heart patients on the waiting lists will die due to a shortage of organs. The number of available transplant organs has not increased in spite of the high success rates.

The medical community must also recognize a problem with economies of scale. There are many hospitals competing for a finite supply of transplantable organs. Many hospitals have created duplicate facilities, and excess staffs, performing only a small number of transplants. The proficiency of the staffs can be seriously questioned, since only a limited number of procedures are performed annually. Patients should question success rates of all institutions prior to considering a transplant. Regional transplant centers should be established to maximize the probability of success. The current trend of establishing new transplant centers has a serious unfavorable escalating effect upon transplant costs.

♡ Cardiac Biopsies

After a transplant, many tests are conducted to determine the effectiveness of the drugs, and the body's reaction to the new organ. Since the body's immune system is constantly attempting to reject the organ, the dosages are adjusted depending upon the results of the cardiac biopsies.

The frequency of the biopsies varies, depending upon the time from the transplant. After my transplant, biopsies were conducted weekly for the first month, and are now (one year from the transplant) scheduled every three months.

The biopsies always cause apprehension, since they are a report card on how well you are doing. I always dread the procedure.

The operation is performed in a catherization laboratory or Operating Room. The skin on the right side of the neck is cleansed. The patient is given a local anesthetic, causing a stinging sensation. A tiny incision is made, and the physician inserts an instrument called a bioptome into the large vein in the neck.

The bioptome is gradually inserted and advanced through the vein until it reaches the heart. The bioptome has a set of pinchers that snip about five small samples of the heart, about the size of a pinhead. After each piece is harvested, the bioptome is withdrawn, and reinserted.

The specimens are sent to a lab and examined under microscopes, and reviewed for any signs of rejection. If rejection is suspected, medication is generally increased. If no rejection is suspected for several biopsies, the period between biopsies is increased.

The procedure itself is not painful, except for the discomfort of the anesthetic being administered. You are conscious, and can feel a sensation of pressure as the bioptome is being inserted. You do not feel any pain when the samples are being taken of the new heart, since the surrounding nerves are not connected to the body.

♡ Denervation

When a new heart is transplanted into a body, all nerves are severed. Normally, two nerve systems affect the performance of the heart: the sympathetic nervous system and the parasympathetic nervous system. Together, the systems jointly control most of the performance of the heart.

When you begin to exercise, or come under stress, the sympathetic nervous system tells the heart to beat faster, and the change begins to take place almost instantaneously. When exercise is complete, and stress lessened, the parasympathetic nervous system tells the heart to slow down. Again, the change begins almost immediately.

After a transplant, the heart does not operate in the same manner. The heart will beat at a faster rate at rest (about 100 times per minute, or about a million times per week), because it is no longer controlled by the central nervous system. Instead, the heart rate is controlled by hormones that are circulating in the blood (adrenaline).

An increase in exercise may cause the adrenal gland to secrete more adrenaline that may not be detected by the heart for several minutes. Similarly, when exercise is stopped, the heart will continue to beat at a high rate for a considerable amount of time until the adrenaline level is decreased. After the transplant, it is important that sudden changes in activity levels be avoided, as well as activities that could cause a sudden change in blood pressure (such as use of a whirlpool or sauna).

After a transplant, it is important that other signs be noticed that could indicate rejection, such as elevated temperature. Generally, a heart transplant patient will not have pain, or any sensation that usually would accompany heart failure. The risk of coronary heart disease also increases dramatically after a transplant, for unknown reasons.

The development of the disease appears to be accelerated, and it is highly recommended that a low salt, and low cholesterol diet be followed subsequent to the transplant.

♡ Side Effects

After a transplant, there is a delicate balance that must be maintained to prevent rejection of the transplanted organ, coupled with a regimen that will cause minimal harm to other organs.

For about three months after the transplant, I experienced numbness in my feet, and regular sessions of severe leg and hand cramps. The cramps were especially bothersome, since there was no particular pattern, and they were very painful. I was concerned that my entire life would contain daily sessions of pain that could not be curbed through medication. In addition, I didn't know why, how, and when they would occur.

Finally, during one of the biopsies, I mentioned the dilemma to one of the male nurses. He suggested that the high level of cyclosporine, the major antirejection drug, may have increased the need for additional magnesium in my system. The advise was a God-send. Within several days, the episodes with the cramps subsided.

Fluid retention is also a common problem, especially if a moderate to high dosage of steroids, such as prednisone is taken. The steroids also cause an increased appetite. The fluids can be regulated by taking lasix, a diruretic. Unfortunately, the use of lasix to flush the fluids also causes an imbalance of potassium, that helps to promote the electrical system in the body. If an imbalance occurs, there is additional need for a potassium supplement.

♡ The Donor

I am often asked if I think of the donor, or if I ever contacted their family.

I think of the donor every day, and often wonder what type of person he was, what he looked like, if he had a family, his likes and dislikes and his interests. I wonder about his hobbies, his religion, his childhood, and the thoughts which passed through his mind during the last few seconds of his life.

I pray for him and his family, and know that our God gave him renewed life through my body, just as I was given renewed life through his heart.

I wrote his family a letter several months after the transplant, and forwarded the letter to the organ procurement agency. It will be their decision to forward the letter, based on their evaluation of the donor's family, and what they feel will be in the best interest of that family.

If they feel the donor's family will benefit by knowing that their loved one has continued to prolong the life of someone, the letter will probably be forwarded. If they feel the family will be grieved by being reminded of the death of their loved one, the letter will not be forwarded. My name, address and other personal data will be deleted from the note to insure confidentiality.

The feelings of the donor's family are always of prime consideration in the transplant process.

Heart transplant patients are constantly reminded of the transplant because, unlike the kidney or liver, or pancreas, you can feel the heart constantly beating. Each hour, my donor heart beats 6,000 times, or about 1,000,000 times per week. I tell the various audiences of the rhythmic, constant reminder.

I often hold my grandson to my chest, and watch his eyes as he listens to the constant beating of my heart. One day, Sebastian will realize that through the love of a stranger, and his family, his grandfather was able to be with him within minutes of his birth.

I often wonder whether the donor and I would have been friends, had we known each other. I wonder if he had a family, and whether he liked to play basketball, or had a son. Had he experienced the thrill of seeing his daughter in a ballet recital, or seen his son play in a soccer game? Had he ever been to the beach, water skiied or taught his son and daughter how to drive a car? Was he an accountant, an engineer, a factory worker, or a lawyer?

I will be eternally grateful to the donor and his family for their gift of life. I want to take advantage of the extended life to spread the word about organ donation. My donor and I are partners.

♡ A Donor Family

About six months after the transplant, I was attending a group discussion on brain death at a local hospital. Toward the end of the meeting, I was approached by hospital personnel, and asked if I could take a few minutes and discuss transplantation with a family who had consented to have their loved one's organs donated. I had never done anything similar to that before, but eagerly agreed.

When you have a heart transplant, you often wonder why you were selected to live, when others die. After the discussion, I thought perhaps that God had spared me to talk with the grieving family of the donor. I was riding home thinking of the family, and whether I had said and done the right thing.

The discussion with the donor's family was very intense. I asked the nursing supervisor if she would accompany me during the meeting. We entered a small room. There were about eight people in the room including the donor's parents, spouse and siblings. The nursing supervisor formally introduced me to the family, and I began to tell them about the great courage, love and generosity they showed by considering organ donation. I told them of the miracle of transplantation, and how it had improved the quality of my life, and how I was able to do activities which would have been impossible without the transplant.

I asked them about their loved one, who had died in an accident. I was told that they were a very caring person who enjoyed life, and had been a good person. I assured them that their loved one would never die, and could help many others, even in death. I told them of the my friends who had died waiting for a heart donor, and the numerous patients I had seen on dialysis machines, and how their lives might be improved with transplanted organs. I told them of others who would benefit from cornea transplants.

I kept stressing that their loved one would concur with their decision, since they had been a caring person. As I spoke, I noticed relief in the eyes of the donor's relatives. I think they wanted to be assured that they had made the right decision. Certainly, it had probably been one of the most difficult of their lives.

When we were talking, we all began to weep. I felt great empathy toward the family. What a traumatic decision they had made, but they found solace that they were going to be helping others.

When all of their questions were answered, I once again confirmed that their decision represented the greatest showing of love possible. I walked over to the mother and hugged her, and again shook hands with the others in the room. The nursing supervisor and I walked into an empty room, and she began to cry. She commented that she had never witnessed a discussion like she had just seen. I felt that I had done some good, and had helped the donor's family realize

♡ Dusty Michelle Futrall

I never met Dusty, but I feel that I knew her. I met her mother, Pat Marsh, during a presentation made to a class of nursing students at the Mideast Ohio Vocational School in Zanesville. Her mom worked for LOOP (Lifeline of Ohio Organ Procurement), the organ procurement agency for Southeast Ohio.

During her part of the presentation, Pat mentioned that her daughter had been killed in an automobile accident, and prior to the accident, had expressed a desire to be an organ donor. Unfortunately, a series of foul ups and neglect had prevented her from accomplishing her wish.

I asked Pat if she could tell me about her daughter because Dusty's story deserved to be told. Pat graciously consented. Perhaps Dusty's experience would help to save someone's life.

Dusty was life personified...a homecoming queen...cheerleader...a superb athlete (Captain of her high school basketball and volleyball teams) who enjoyed scuba diving. She was pretty with sparkling dark eyes and dark hair...fluent in Spanish and an honor student. She enjoyed classical music. She had everything going for her, and enjoyed life to its fullest. She had already completed her freshman year at Ohio State University in Columbus, and was looking forward to continuing her studies in marine biology.

She had studied the subject of organ and tissue donation for several years, and had signed her driver's license and advised her mother that if she was ever in an accident, she wanted to help others through the donation of her tissues and organs. Dusty was a giver in life...not a taker.

Dusty was 19 years old when she and two friends were returning from an evening at Kent State University in the early morning of August 24, 1990. Dusty was driving her Jeep westbound on the Ohio turnpike, on the way to her home in Cleveland. No one is certain what happened that evening, although a truck driver following the Jeep reported the vehicle began to swerve in and out of its lane. It suddenly veered off the left side of the road, and smashed into a guard rail with high impact. Dusty was thrown from the vehicle.

She was not wearing a seat belt, although, on hundreds of occasions, she had badgered her passengers to buckle their seat belts. The car had stopped earlier, and coffee had been purchased. It is conjecture that her seat belt was not fastened because she was trying to drink her coffee and stay awake.

Dusty was rushed to a hospital in a small town near Cleveland. She died shortly thereafter. Her father was at the hospital when she left this earth. Her mom, Pat, was rushing from Columbus to be with her daughter, but Dusty expired prior to Pat reaching Cleveland. Pat, remembering the many conversations, asked Dusty's father if the medical professionals had asked, as required by federal law, if Dusty could be an organ or tissue donor.

The doctors had not asked, and an autopsy had already begun, rendering all tissues and organs unsuitable for transplant. A totally sterile environment was not maintained during the autopsy.

One of Dusty's fondest wishes had not been fulfilled. She had done everything correctly. She had signed her donor card, expressed her desires with her family and friends, and maintained a healthy and active life style. Her tissues would have improved the quality of life for others who needed them.

Another tragedy was the attitude of the attending physician, who was later asked why he did not ask about organ donation. He flippantly remarked that "I didn't want to screw around with it." How many lives were adversely affected by the callous attitude of the doctor? A simple question may have restored sight to a blind person, or improved the life of someone else.

The family can not always be expected to remember the desires of the deceased. We are caught up in the shock of seeing a loved one die.

The emotions at the moment generally do not facilitate clear thinking. The health care professionals must take the leadership role in asking the grieving families about organ donations.

I have had several discussions with Dusty's mother regarding the denial of her daughter's wishes, as well as the doctor's comments. She has said that she will always be haunted because her daughter's wishes were not carried out. I have tried to explain that she could not have done anything differently. Pat believes in organ transplantation, and continues to make presentations to students and other groups to encourage organ donation.

The memory of Dusty Futrall should encourage all of us to state our wishes again and again, and to help our health care professionals to do all aspects of their job. The great sacrifice and gift of love that they had given.

♡ Pete Petoniak

Several months after the transplant, I realized the story of transplants and the lack of organ donors had to be publicized.

I had been disappointed when I attempted to renew my driver's license, and had not been asked about organ donations. I later wrote to the Department of Motor Vehicles who stated the law had been changed to accommodate a change mandated by the federal Government. The new law was attempting to install a new national driver's license, and information regarding organ donation had been eliminated from the back of the license, necessitating a sticker on the front of the license, and a separate form indicating consent. The new law increased the probability that applicants would not be asked about organ donation, depending upon the attitude of the state license bureau personnel.

Personnel at the agency stated they always asked, which was questionable when any other friends noticed that they also had not been asked. I was disappointed that Lifeline of Ohio Organ Procurement (LOOP) as well as the elected legislators allowed such an important piece of legislation to pass without an understanding of the consequences.

I contacted Pete Petoniak, Program Director for WHIZ, the local radio and tv station, and appeared on his noon program LIVE AT NOON to discuss organ transplants as well the change in the law.

Pete later provided help and encouragement in writing and recording about 15 Public Service Announcements. He played them regularly, as well as sending copies to other stations in Ohio. I had asked LOOP for samples of announcements, and was told that only 2 were available. We also recorded them for distribution. Pete's assistance and interest resulted in a significant increase of public awareness in Southeast Ohio.

I later wrote to the National Association of Broadcasters, informing them of the community service programs of WHIZ. They later requested information, including video tapes that were proposed to be played at the national convention. The station was a Crystal Award winner for 1990, only 1 of 10 stations in the United States (out of 10,000) to receive the honor.

♡ Golfing

I had always been a lousy golfer, and had always been somewhat bewildered that I had been unable to master the game. I became so frustrated, and decided that I did not have the time, or money to devote to developing the skills required to be a good golfer.

Barb had purchased a good set of Jack Nicklaus clubs for me on our first anniversary in 1968, when she worked at Brunswick Corporation in Muskegon, Michigan. The clubs were about the only part of my game that was decent, and as the years rolled on, my game became more erratic. I finally decided that it was probably better, and less expensive, if I retired from recreational competition until I was ready to make a firm commitment. The clubs went into a corner of the garage, and were moved several times around the Midwest when I was changing jobs.

The only action that the clubs saw was when I peered out of the window on several occasions and saw David swinging wildly in the back yard, driving stones into the woods. I purchased a set of little metal clubs for him to practice his stone hitting. He was about six years old.

When we moved to Zanesville, David was 10 years old. One afternoon, I was perusing the garage and noticed the golf clubs in the corner. I decided that I was either going to sell the clubs, or devote ample effort to improve my game, but the decision would depend upon David.

I asked him if he would like to learn how to golf on a real golf course.

He stated that he was not sure, so I made him an offer...We would go to the golf course, and golf 9 holes on a little par 3 near our home. The deal was quite simple...if he liked the game, I would buy him a junior set and we would continue to go golfing. If he did not have a good time...I would sell the clubs.

We went golfing and had a wonderful time. His game steadily improved, and through some miracle...so did mine! We enjoy golfing together...he loves to drive the cart, and he has mastered an activity that he'll be able to enjoy all of his life.

I'm glad that he was willing to learn back in 1984.

♡ John Garrett and the Little Engine That Could
Written by Becky Leasure
CCU Supervisor, Bethesda Hospital

Sometime during our preschool years, our parents read to us the story entitled The Little Engine That Could. In addition to being a fun story, although we didn't realize it, this was one of our earliest lessons in positive thinking. For those of you who have forgotten the story, it goes something like this.

There was a train whose job whose job it was to haul loads of toys to the children on the other side of the mountain. One day as the train pulled into the engine house, four of its wheels fell off. The engineer of the train, who was a clown, began to cry. He was upset because he would not be able to take the toys across the mountain to the children.

Well, the engine house was full of train engines....a sleek diesel engine, an enormous freight engine, a rusty-dusty engine, and a little blue switch engine. In an attempt to solve his problem, the clown tried to get one of the engines to pull his load of toys over the mountain. Each engine, in turn, had an excuse.

The sleek diesel engine explained that he was a passenger train and he would not think of pulling a shabby little train of toys. The enormous freight engine described how he pulled hundreds of oil tanks, important machinery cars, and loads of lumber. He would feel just plain silly pulling a little trainload of toys. The rusty-dusty engine had spots in front of its headlights, its whistle was stuck, and it wasn't well enough to make the trip. Last of all, the little blue switch engine had never been out of the railroad yard and didn't know if he could.

The clown hopped aboard the little blue switch engine and begged him to try. The little blue switch engine responded with, "I think I can. I think I can." As the little blue switch engine started up the mountain, the going became tougher and tougher.

"I think I can. I hope I can." said the little blue switch engine. Next, they crossed over a rickety bridge; half way across, the bridge swayed and splintered. "I think I can. I think I can." said the little blue switch engine.

As they reached the other side of the bridge, it collapsed into firewood. Next, they came to a tunnel filled with smoke. The little blue engine was fearful that they might wreck. But, the only way to go was ahead, so the little blue switch engine sputtered and coughed through the tunnel, all the way saying, "I think I can. I think I can."

After passing through the tunnel, there was a big bear on the track, who stood and growled fiercely. The clown urged the little blue switch engine on. As they came closer to the bear, he ran off the track.

As the little blue switch engine came nearer the top of the mountain, he called out, "I think I can. I think I can. I know I can." As he rushed down the other side of the mountain, he shouted with joy, "I thought I could! I thought I could! I knew I could! I knew I could!"

I really don't know if John Garrett knows the story of The Little Engine That Could. I do know that he has learned well the lesson of positive thinking. Since his first heart attack and triple bypass surgery in 1980, John has had multiple obstacles to contend with on his "track of life".

During 1989, John was hospitalized for several months while being evaluated, and waiting on the possibility of a new heart. On two occasions during his extensive wait, John was notified of an available heart; only to be informed that the donor heart was not suitable for transplant. Of course John was discouraged, but he never gave up hope (I think I can. I hope I can).

John spent a portion of his hospitalization in Bethesda's Coronary Care Unit; he was with us from June 15, 1989 to August 25, 1989. During this time, the staff shared John's setbacks, but also his triumphs.

One particularly difficult time for John was when he received word that he had been taken off Ohio State University's list of persons waiting to receive a heart. It was like a bridge on his "track of life" that came tumbling down about him. But, like the little blue switch engine, John saw only one solution, and that was to go forward.

Moving ahead, he worked towards, and was successful, in adding his name at Vanderbilt University Hospital in Nashville, Tennessee.

Also on the side of triumphs, one particularly happy time for John was when he walked his daughter down the aisle of the Bethesda Hospital Chapel. This was a specific goal that he had set for himself. (I think I can. I know I can).

Finally, on October 9, 1989 John underwent heart transplant surgery at Vanderbilt University Medical Center. The day following surgery, even while still on the respirator, John's attitude was definitely, "I thought I could. I knew I could."

During this past year, John has done well on his "track to recovery". There will always be some broken bridges, bears, or smokey tunnels on John's track. Currently, John must return to Vanderbilt University every few weeks for testing for possible rejection. He also must maintain a strict medication regime. Yes, John Garrett still experiences some days where depression and discouragement creep in, but his overall attitude is "I knew I could! I knew I could!"

John continues his positive attitude as he speaks to individuals, and to groups regarding the merits of organ donation. John's goal is to make a positive contribution, and a positive difference to mankind. So, if you think things aren't going so well for you, just think of John Garrett and The Little Engine That Could. You will find the positive power to move forward on your own "track of life".

(Note: I do not know the author of the original story of The Little Engine That Could.)

♡ Sebastian David Luu

Sebastian Luu is our grandson, and holds a very special place in our hearts. He was born on February 25, 1990 at Bethesda Hospital in Zanesville, the son of our daughter Beth and son-in-law Thuy.

One of the exciting things about Sebastian is Barb and I were there when he was born, and we were able to hold him when he was about

15 minutes old. Without the heart transplant, it is very doubtful that I would have lived long enough to see him, to hold him, to push him in his stroller, to make funny noises and watch his expressions, his smiles and his sounds. I would not have been able to see him walk.

The night before he was born, I went to the video store to rent a few movies. It was bitter cold, and when I came home I asked Beth if she and Thuy wanted to watch the movies. Beth didn't feel well, and advised me to watch the first movie alone, and she would perhaps feel better in a few hours. At the end of the movie, Beth and Thuy advised me Beth was having contractions, and they were heading to the hospital.

About seven hours later, the miracle of birth occurred, and we were presented with the cutest little fellow I've ever seen.

I call him the little man. He seems to enjoy his visits to our home. His eyes are sparkling, and he smiles easily. He loves to play Pattycake. All you have to do is to say "Pattycake" and he quickly starts clapping his hands. He took his first five unaided steps when he was ten months old. I know it doesn't seem like a big deal to most people that my grandson can walk, and play Pattycake, but I've come to appreciate the little things in life. We all have so much to be thankful for, and they're not the big, glamorous awards like the Oscars and the Emmys.

I look forward to the little man's visits to our home, and hope that I'm able to experience many more of them. I want to buy him a bicycle, just as his great grandfather bought bikes for his Mom and Uncle Dave. It will be a great thrill when the training wheels are removed, and he begins to ride up and down the sidewalk.

♡ Bravery and Courage

People often comment that it takes great courage to have a heart transplant. I always comment that the people with courage are the donors and their families, and our friends who face each day with hope.

♡ Mike and Jan Tandy

I was once interviewed for an article in our local newspaper entitled "Getting to Know You". One of the questions concerned people whom we most admired. I answered that I most admired people with severe mental or physical handicaps who do their very best. At the time of the interview, I was thinking of several people at our church.

One person was a gentleman, about my age, who had once been very active in the community, until struck with a debilitating illness which left him unable to do many things that are a part of our daily lives. He accepted his ordeal with great determination, and could be seen each Sunday at church regardless of the weather. Others were scared to venture out on a winter Sunday morning to attend church, but Chuck Vonada was always there. He was a true example of courage. His wife, Ellen, and daughters would help him in and out, and to the car. I never heard him complain. I admired him and his determination.

I was also thinking of Mike and Jan Tandy when the subject of courage was discussed. Mike and Jan were the parents of 5 children. Two (Casey and Pam) were from Mike's previous marriage and two (Bart and Bret) were from Jan's previous marriage. Together, they had a son, Keith who is now 17 years old.

Keith had developed an illness which left him unable to think and function as a normal person. He attended a school during the day, beginning when he was three years old, for children with special needs. Jan, Mike and Keith's brothers and sister provided much love and support for Keith. He attended church, sometimes staying in the kitchen during the services. He had a strong affinity to plastic lids found on coffee and food cans. He carefully examined each lid and would look at them from all angles. We don't know why he liked lids so much...only Keith and God know for sure. Jan and Mike's friends save lids for Keith...he has quite a collection.

Bart, Keith's brother, was his best friend. They had more than a normal brother relationship. Bart was very patient with Keith and accepted him with great brotherly love and compassion. Keith would wait patiently for Bart when he left home, and seemed to wait patiently for his return. One night, Bart did not come home, and he would never come home, and today, Jan leaves a candle burning in his bedroom window.

Bart had attended a party with a friend, and the friend asked Bart to drive him home. They were in strange territory, and Bart was driving a strange car on strange roads. He approached a busy road, early in the morning. Bart did not notice the stop sign at the dark intersection. His car began to cross the road.

Suddenly a four wheel drive utility vehicle crashed into the driver's side compartment at 55 miles per hour. Bart's life ended suddenly. Many of his dreams would be unfulfilled. Jan and Mike had lost a beloved son and Keith had lost his best friend.

Mike and Jan have to be among the most courageous of all people, to have endured Bart's sudden death. They face each day with optimism despite the loss of their son. They continue to cherish the moments they shared with Bart, and the sixteen years they had together. They continue to care for Keith with the greatest amount of affection. They are among the bravest people that I've ever known.

During my illness, the mail brought cards and letters of encouragement from Mike and Jan, together with pictures of their granddaughter, Megan, who I had taught to swim.

Megan's picture adorned the wall of the hospital room during the long wait for the transplant.

♡ Community Support

Approximately six months after the transplant, National Organ and Tissue Donor Awareness came during the last week of April. I attempted to publicize the week, and was met with a great deal of support from the local community, as well as some unexpected, but welcomed, news.

One of the local hospitals, Good Samaritan Medical Center, sponsored a luncheon symposium on organ donation and advertised in the local newspaper. They asked me to speak, as well as Jenny Hoover, a transplant coordinator from LOOP, the Lifeline of Ohio Organ Procurement agency. Unfortunately, the seminar was sparsely attended. Several members of the McGrawettes, Rita Himmelspach, Mildred Berry, and Janet Finley, one of my nurses from Bethesda Hospital, Alison Yusufzai, some family friends, Barbara Taylor and Gretchen Sayre and Joe Kelly from Zane Trace Church of Christ, attended the meeting.

Later that week, I spoke before a meeting of the Ohio Retired Teachers Association and a conference of church clergy.

I also went to various merchants on Maple Avenue, the major

thoroughfare in Zanesville who had marquees. Each agreed to display a message informing the public of National Organ and Tissue Donor Awareness Week. I later sent thank you notes to each of the businesses for their support.

If the firm had a national affiliation, I also sent a letter of thanks to the home offices, letting them know of the support that they were giving to the local community. The President of one company, Ashland Oil, replied that he fully supported organ transplantation. Mr. John Pettus, reported that one of his Vice Presidents had received a heart transplant, and he was well aware of the "Gift of Life".

The local NBC affiliate WHIZ, and a dynamic Program Manager, Pete Petoniak, helped to record Public Service Announcements, and aired them regularly. The TIMES RECORDER, the local newspaper, also ran several articles on organ transplants. The publicity was well received by the community. Many friends commented they had noticed the extensive penetration by the media.

♡ Simon Keith

Several weeks after the transplant, I was reading a SPORTS ILLUSTRATED magazine, and came upon an article regarding a rookie professional soccer player named Simon Keith. Simon played soccer for the Cleveland Crunch of the Major Indoor Soccer League.

The article told an amazing story. Simon Keith had undergone a heart transplant several years before, and had been selected as the number one draft choice of the Crunch in the 1989 amateur draft. He was the only active professional athlete in the world who had undergone a heart transplant.

Simon downplayed the effect of the transplant, and had proven that post transplant activities need not be curtailed. After the transplant, he had been chosen as a first team All Big West Conference at the University of Nevada at Las Vegas for two consecutive years.

I was very impressed with his attitude, and wrote him a short note expressing my admiration of his courage. I commented that I wanted to come to a Crunch game sometime in the future to meet him, and asked for a schedule of remaining games. Several days later, there was a message on my answering machine. Simon Keith had called. We tried to make connections, without success. Finally, a member of the Media Relations staff called. We made arrangements to attend a future game.

Barb and I, together with David and two of his friends, Tim Kronenbitter and Jason Bone, journeyed to Richfield, a suburb of Cleveland, to attend a game. The Crunch defeated the San Diego Sockers in overtime. After the game, we were permitted into the runway leading to the locker room. Simon soon appeared.

Amid the confusion, I told him he was an outstanding example to transplant patients, as well as the young people in our country. I also asked if we could have pictures taken with David and his friends, as well as myself. I also asked if I could utilize him in promoting organ donation, as well as youth soccer in Zanesville. He posed for pictures as we continued to talk about the transplant and the effect of cyclosporine. He asked if I ever "Got the Shakes", one of the normal side effects. I told him occasionally.

The discussion concluded when he said "John, I have your telephone number, and you have mine. Let's keep in touch." He disappeared into the tunnel with a crowd of reporters. I later learned that Simon was probably the most widely known professional player in North America, and had done extensive interviews on ESPN as well as scores of newspapers. I found him to be a considerate and caring individual.

♡ Frank Galasso

Frank Galasso was a plant manager with McGraw-Edison in Zanesville. He was married to Claudia and had three children: Frank Jr., Paula and Michelle. Frank was a wonderful and devoted Christian and family man, and a brilliant business person.

He was a former accountant from Pennsylvania, who migrated into the operations side of the business. I use to kid Frank that one of the true miracles in the world was how anything ever made it out the shipping door at Zanesville. The plant was in the shape of a Z, with extensive material handling required to manufacture the product. The antiquated equipment made quality and scheduling goals extremely hard to meet. Frank accepted all challenges.

I considered Frank Galasso to be the best manager in our division... bar none.

Frank was a great friend. Our offices were across from each other, and we had many meetings together on a variety of activities. More important, he was always available if I had personal concerns, and I was there if he had a problem. I once told Claudia that we meet thousands of people during our lifetimes, and there are a few that stand out above the rest. Frank was that type of person. He was a tough taskmaster, but he was fair. The man had integrity.

Frank eventually left McGraw-Edison and moved to Phoenix. On the day that he left, I wrote him a note telling him that he had helped me in so many ways. I cried.

He would call me after I entered the hospital, and after I had returned to Zanesville. I enjoyed his calls. One day, he called and I was out at the grocery, and he talked at length with Barb. He told her that he loved Phoenix, and was feeling great. I was sorry that I had missed his call.

Several days later, we received another call about Frank. He had died. I wept. Another of the truly wonderful friends in my life was gone. I asked myself...why Frank and not me?

♡ Speeches

I am frequently asked to address civic, church and school groups to promote organ donation. Of all the types of groups addressed, I enjoy the school programs to be the most challenging.

I recently addressed a group of 180 students in Frazeysburg, Ohio. The students and teachers were seated in the auditorium, and I told them of the long wait for a transplant, the support of my family and the many cards and prayers of my friends. I told them of the brave 34 year old Tennessee man and his family whose gift of life had enabled me to live.

We spoke of the need to maintain a healthy lifestyle free of cigarettes and drugs, and the need for them to take care of their bodies. After the speech, there were numerous questions concerning the cost of the transplant and the operation itself. I was fascinated by the insight of the students, and told them the shortage of organs and the development of artificial organs would be solved by their generation, not mine. Afterwards,

I received numerous thank-you notes from the faculty and students. I was very gratified by the interest shown by the young generation.

I told the students that life is very short, and to follow several rules in life including:

    Love your mother and father.
    Love your brothers and sisters.
    Take care of your bodies.
    Don't give up.
    Don't do drugs.
    Trust God.
    Love God.

♡ Rules for the Game of Life
A Man's Advise to His Son

When our family was living in Franklin Tennessee, I noticed an advertisement in the NASHVILLE MAGAZINE for Williams Printing Company. The advertisement had a lot of meaning to me, and has continued to play a part in my life. I have made many copies for friends:

I am giving you the ball, son, and naming you quarterback for your team in the game of life.

I am your coach, so I'll give it to you straight. There is only one schedule to play.

It lasts all your life but consists of only one game.

It is a long game with no time outs and no substitutions

You play the whole game- all your life.

You'll have a great backfield.

You're calling the signals but the other three fellows in the backfield with you have great reputations.

They are named Faith, Hope, and Love. You'll work behind a truly powerful line. End to end it consists of Honesty, Loyalty, Devotion to Duty, Self-Respect, Study, Cleanliness, and Good Behavior.

The goal posts are the pearly gates of Heaven.

God is the referee and sole official.

He makes all the rules and there is no appeal from them.

There is also an important ground rule.

It is "as ye would that men should do to you, do ye also to them likewise"!

Here is the ball.

It is your immortal soul!

Hold on to it.

Now, son, get in there and let's see what you can do with it.

♡ Notes from Frazeysburg Students

Mr. Garret

Thank you for an intriguing speech. It was fascinating.

Brandi

Thank You Mr. Garrett

I learned a lot from the speech. And now I know what people go through.

Christa

Dear John

Thank you for the speech. I really enjoyed it. I learned more about a heart transplant. I hope to see you some time in the future. Tell your family I said hi. Thank you again. Your new friend.

Erica

To Mr. Garrett

Thank you so much for coming. I am glad you are better. Come again.

From Heather !!!

Thank you so much

Mr. Garret - Thank you for your time. I found your speech interesting. I find you a very brave man. I wont forget you. May God be with you and your family.

Love in Christ Stephanie

Thanks Alot!

Mr. Garrett - I really enjoyed your visit. I learned a lot from you. People's life stories when they're battling for their life interests me very much.

Your friend
Amy

Dear Mr. Garrett,

Thank you very much for coming to talk to us. We got a lot of interesting facts and I really enjoyed it. Pleases come back and visit again.

Your friend Stephanie

Thanks Mr. Garrett

Thanks for coming in to our school and teaching us about heart transplants. I learned that transplants can happen to people all over.

Love,
Matthew

Dear Mr. Garrett

I really enjoyed your speech. I thought it was very interesting. I think that I would consider you a very brave man. I don't think that I would have been that brave. I think that it was a good idea to have you come and talk to us.

Your friend, Heather

Thank you Mr. Garrett

I enjoyed the program a lot. It was very interesting. I wish you good luck and success with your new heart.

From: Roy

Mr. Garrett,

Thank you very much for taking the time out of your busy secual to come and tell us about your life. I enjoyed it very much.

Thanks again
Manda

Mr. John Garrett,

I really enjoyed your speech about your life. It seems that you've had a very hard time. Now I'm going to exercise and watch what I eat from now on. Like you said you are a very lucky man. Thanks for coming to our school. Good luck in the future. C-U-later.

Your friend,
Dustan

P.S. Tell your wife and kids I said Hi.

Dear Mr. Garrett

I really enjoyed your presentation. It was interesting to me because my grandfather just had a heart attack this past December. I think it's amazing that you're still alive. You gave us great advise that we can still use. As my grandpa told me, "God must still have something planed for me" I think God still has something planned for you.

The person who wrote this letter,
Jessica

Mr. Garrett

Thank you very much for sharing your story. I thought it was very interesting and I think you are brave and have more courage than anyone I know. I think your family is great and very supportive and I hope one day I could get to meet them. I will always remember you and the thoughts you put in me and all your courage. I will watch on the Today program and hope to see you and maybe your family. I hope you remember all of us in your heart.

Sincerely,
Jason

Dear Mr. Garett

Thank you for coming. I learned a lot from you, and I hope you come back! The kid sitting in the second row asking all those questions!!

Your friend

Dear John,

Thank you for your sermon. I enjoyed greatly. I thought it was very interesting when you were talking about waiting for your heart, it must have been hard, huh. Well, gotta go but good luck with your new heart!

Your friend, Corey

Mr. Garrett,

I would like to thank you for taking the time to stop and talk to us about your life. It really got me thinking about my heart. Because I've never really thought about it. Thanks again.

Yours truly, Mariann

Dear John,

Thank you!!! Thank you for coming in and talking to us. It was very interesting and enjoyable listening to you. I hope I will be able to read your book it also sound exciting. I hope your heart transplant works good and you have a long happy life.

Thank you Amy

Dear Mr. Garret,

Thank you. I really enjoyed that thing about your heart transplant. It was very interesting.

Your friend, Missy

John Garret

I liked your speech. I learned a lot. You must have had a long wait for a heart. Thank you for coming!

Sincerely, Brad

♡ Drinking Pepsi Cola

One of life's small pleasures is the ability to drink a Pepsi Cola without being worried. One of the side effects of cardiomyopathy is the inability of the body to dispose of the fluids.

Fluids are carefully monitored. All drinks are measured, with each ounce containing 30 units. A can of pop has 360 units. During the internship, fluid restrictions prevented me from drinking a pop. Ice was calculated carefully, with a conversion to fluid ounces and units. Fluids not consumed on one shift could not be carried over to the next shift, nor could fluids be borrowed from the next shift. I suppose the restrictions would not have bothered me if they were not enforced so strictly. I tried to negotiate, without success. I became thirsty, and craved a drink.

I wanted to drink a Pepsi, but the restrictions placed a premium on the amount of fluids. I pleaded with the doctors to allow extra fluids, figuring the excess fluid could be dealt with diruretics. The physicians maintained an unyielding attitude against any compromise. I had absolutely no control, no input, and was totally ignored by the physicians in Columbus.

Shortly prior to the transplant, I asked one of the surgical team at Vanderbilt if I would have any limitations after the transplant. He said no, and that I would be as good as new. I asked him if I would be able to drink a whole Pepsi, without regard to fluid restrictions. He said I could drink as many Pepsis as I wanted to consume. I bet him a 16 ounce Pepsi on the outcome of the World Series. I'm still waiting to collect.

♡ Muhammad Ali

I never talked with Mohammad Ali, but I had an opportunity of observing him for several days in 1975. He was training for a championship match in Cleveland against Chuck Wepner.

Boxing fans will recognize Check Wepner as the boxer portrayed by Sylvester Stallone in the Rocky series. Chuck was a club fighter, and known in boxing circles as the Bayonne Bleeder, for obvious reasons. His tendency to absorb maximum punishment with his body and face was probably his greatest asset. His boxing skills had been maximized to the fullest, and he was suddenly thrust into a title match with the greatest boxer of all time.

My brother, Joe, and I would drive to the Coliseum to watch the boxers train. Usually, Wepner would train earlier in the morning, and Joe and I almost came to know Chuck on a first-name basis. We were usually the only ones in the gym except for several sparing partners, Chuck's manager and his trainer.

After watching Chuck train and talking with him, we knew his heart, and not his skills, was his greatest asset. Chuck hit the heavy bag with authority, but his lack of hand speed was evident. We wondered if Ali would taunt and punish him.

After Chuck would train, a crowd would begin to form, waiting for Ali to appear. Network and local television personalities, newspaper reporters, and assorted hangers-on filled the gym. Suddenly, excitement reached a fever pitch, as a large muscular fighter with broad shoulders, a beautiful face and body entered the gym. His entire entourage was there, including his trainer, Angelo Dundee, a full stable of sparring partners, and Boudini Brown, his emotional guru.

Ali trained effortlessly. His hand and foot speed were unbelievably fast, and he bantered with the crowd as the sparring partners attempted to club him with tremendous force. He managed to slip most of the punches, or block them with his gloves. His moves were effortless. I knew that Chuck Wepner was in for a rough evening, and would absorb a lot of punishment.

After the sessions, Ali would stand in a corner and answer questions for the crowd, as well as the media. People would hold their children up, and Ali would hug and kiss them. He smiled easily and joked with the crowd. He posed with various fund raising groups, and would hold posters promoting various causes in Cleveland. At one point, I noticed him talking with a gentleman, smile and nod his head.

I watched the man leave the ring apron, and move to a place near the ring. He approached a young girl who appeared to be about 13 years old. It appeared that the little girl may have been retarded, since her glasses were quite thick, and she had a bewildered look on her face. Her dress was slightly unorthodox.

The man took her hand, and led her up the steps in the corner opposite the corner where Ali was continuing his conversation. He held the ropes up as the little girl climbed through the strands. The man led the teen across the ring, and upon reaching Ali, tapped him on the shoulder. Ali turned, smiled at the man and looked down at the little girl, and smiled at her.

The little girl looked up at Ali. Suddenly her face was filled with fear. She immediately ran to the opposite corner, and huddled into a fetal position. Ali quickly followed her, and upon reaching the corner, dropped down to his knees, and began to speak softly to the girl. He put his arms around her. She listened to him, and looked at his face.

She began to smile. Ali continued to smile and talk with her. He soon stood up, and the little girl held his hand as they walked across the ring. Many pictures were taken. Ali was resting on one of his knees with his arm around the little girl. They were both smiling. After the session, Ali kissed her on the cheek, and gave her a final hug.

I could hardly believe what I had witnessed. One of the most powerful men in the world had expressed a simple, yet monumental act of love and kindness. I will never forget that moment. Ali will always be one of my heros, and his picture taken on that March afternoon will always be displayed in my home.

A final note. The fight went 15 rounds, and Chuck Wepner absorbed a terrible beating. A friend at a local hospital knew the doctor who sewed the stitches that evening. Chuck was proud that he had managed to survive the onslaught for 15 rounds. I'm proud of Chuck Wepner. His courage and fortitude had served him well.

♡ Ali- The Showman

Ali was one of the best known men in the world. His talent and charisma transcended continents, race, language and economic conditions.

During his training in Cleveland for the Chuck Wepner heavyweight championship fight, Joe and I ventured to the Coliseum to watch him train. He was a spectacular physical specimen, with well defined muscles and broad shoulders.

Ali was so graceful. All his moves were effortless, and he glided about the ring with tremendous speed, taunting his sparring partners to hit him harder (if they could hit him at all). He leaned against the ropes, and rocked back and forth as the sparring partners lunged against him, swinging wildly for his elusive chin. He had a knack for bobbing his head, and the blows would pass within a millimeter of hitting him flush. He would hang against the ropes for the majority of each round, until his manager, Angelo Dundee, yelled "10 seconds".

Ali would bounce off the ropes and hit his sparring partner with six or seven quick jabs to the head. The crowd, appreciative of the skills being exhibited, cheered his moves.

After one session, Ali's sparring partner took a seat between Joe and I. He was a large black man, with a strong chin. He was very engaging to Joe and I, and we began to have a nice conversation. I asked him if he was a professional sparring partner. He said he was also a professional boxer, and was going to be champ when Ali retired.

He said he was undefeated as a professional. He kidded Joe and I, and kiddingly acted as if he would harm us if we were nosy enough to ask how much money he made. I told him we were interested in following his career, and asked where he was from.

He said he was from Easton, Pennsylvania. The boxer was Larry Holmes, who several years after our conversation, became the heavyweight champion of the world. Larry later defeated Ali in a title match. He never achieved the popularity that he deserved. Anyone following Ali would, of course, be compared to Ali, and no one could compare with Ali, the fastest, and most charismatic champion of all time.

Ali was a great showman. After sparring sessions, he would banter with the crowd. Parents would hold up their children for Ali to touch. He would hold the children, and hug and kiss them, and have his picture taken with the youngsters. He never refused a picture or an autograph. He was gracious with his fans. I was watching a legend.

The media was anxious for interviews with Ali. He would consent to interviews, and speak softly as the lights and equipment were being set up by the technicians. When the announcer started to talk, and the lights went on, Ali's face would become distorted, his voice would raise, and it appeared he had lost control of his senses.

He would boast how he would dispose of Chuck Wepner, would beat him within an inch of his life, and how he was a fool to have a fight with the "greatest of all time." Ali was quite convincing as his eyes would dart about the room. When the interview concluded and the camera lights were turned off, Ali immediately began to smile and talk in a normal tone. His eyes would return to normal, and he would hold and kiss more children. Joe and I looked at each other. Ali had convinced millions of people that he was crazy. We were a select few that knew he had succeeded in fooling the world.

♡ Post Transplant Care

Subsequent to a heart transplant, you are constantly aware to how your body is reacting. In order to spot unfavorable trends, you take your temperature, blood pressure and pulse at least two times each day. Any unfavorable sign, such as an elevated temperature will require additional readings.

Each year, an annual physical is performed at Vanderbilt which includes the following routine, as well as other tests:

- Blood pressure- If elevated, there can be an increased probability of stroke or heart attack.
- Electrocardiogram- Indicates the present condition of the heart, and may show an enlargement, electrical defects or rhythm abnormalities. May show possible signs of impaired blood supply or evidence of prior heart attack.
- Stress test- Exercise EKG may reveal signs of hidden heart disease, or confirm cause of cardiac symptoms.
- Echocardiogram- Tests the heart using sound waves. May show faulty heart valves, or enlarged and thickened heart muscle.
- BUN-Blood urea nitrogen; product of protein metabolism; level reflects ability of kidney to excrete the excess, may be high in kidney disease.
- Creatinine-Waste product in blood; is a measure of kidney function; if elevated, may signify kidney disease.
- White Blood Count (WBC) Measures the number of white blood cells; WBC elevated during infection, inflammation, burns, leukemia. Low WBC indicates bone marrow depression-may be present with some viruses, toxic reactions, German measles, infectious hepatitis, and other diseases.

The real heros in the miracle of organ transplantation are the donors and their families who consent to be organ donors. I can not think of a greater expression of love and concern for our fellow humans than to be organ donors.

♡ Shortage

Unfortunately, there is a severe shortage of organ donors in this country... not a shortage of organs, but a shortage of donors. Countless thousands of patients could have an improved quality of life if we could increase the number of organ donations. Approximately 1/3 of the patients on various waiting lists will die due to the low availability of suitable organs.

I have made many speeches to church groups, civic associations, and schools regarding the critical shortage of organs. I hope that I'll be able to address additional groups in the future, and increase donor awareness.

♡ Donor Questions
Attempts to Save Life

One of the major reasons there is a shortage of organ donors is a fear that the medical professionals in charge of saving your life will not do everything possible to save a patient, if they know they are a potential organ donor.

The medical professionals will attempt everything possible to save the life of a potential donor. The professional in charge of saving a life is completely different than the health professional responsible for procuring the organ. There have been many cases where steps taken to save a person's life actually has made the potential organs unsuitable for transplantation.

One of the potential hearts proposed for me was damaged due to a long delay on the part of the donor's family. The family could not decide whether to give permission to be a donor. When they finally reached a decision to allow a transplantation, the heart's condition had deteriorated to a point where transplantation would not have been successful.

It is imperative that all potential donors sign donor cards and discuss their decision with their family. By signing a donor card, the donor relieves the family of the difficult decision of whether to allow transplantation. The decision is made without the emotion and stress of a trauma. In addition, after an accident, a wallet containing a card expressing your desire could easily be lost.

The final decision of becoming a donor rests with the next-of-kin.

Even if a donor card has been signed, the closest blood relative is asked for the final decision.

The final permission for organ donation is given only after death has been pronounced.

♡ How Serious Is The Shortage?

There are over 20,000 people are on waiting lists for organs. Many are sustained only through heavy medications or equipment such as dialysis machines. Other potential patients can not depend on equipment to keep alive, and can survive only with a human transplant. Approximately 1/3 of all heart or liver transplant candidates currently waiting on lists will die due to a lack of available organs. Approximately 1,900 patients died in 1989 waiting for a transplant.

Such a transplanted organ usually comes from someone who has died, and whose family has consented to donate the organ.

♡ Is Pain Involved?

The donor does not feel pain, since all brain functions have stopped.

Brain death occurs when blood ceases to flow to the brain, and the tissue dies. The condition is irreversible. Although the brain has died, other organs and tissues can function for a short time if maintained by a life support system, such as a respirator.

♡ Is The Body Disfigured?

No, the operation is performed under surgical conditions, with a great deal of compassion and care. It involves an abdominal incision that is sutured closed at the completion of the procedure.

The body is treated with much dignity and respect given to any patient undergoing a surgical procedure.

The sterile conditions allow organs to be taken from the body for later transplant. As was discussed in the article of Dusty Futrall, many organs and tissues can be wasted if sterile conditions are not maintained.

♡ How Have Other Donor Families Felt?

Most families feel very positive about the decision to donate organs. Many find solace in having the opportunity of giving others an improved quality of life.

I have discussed organ and tissue donation with many survivors. I have had the opportunity of serving on several panel discussions with a lady whose daughter was a tissue donor. She mentioned, quite eloquently, of the wonderful feeling she has had because her daughter's tissues were donated. She had discussed her daughter's wishes prior to her death. She feels a great deal of good has happened despite the tragic, and premature death of her daughter. She knows that part of her daughter continues to live, and help others.

♡ Legal Authority

The Anatomical Gift Act legalizes organ donation and specifies who may give permission. The order or priority is as follows: spouse, adult son or daughter, either parent, adult brother or sister, or a guardian of the deceased.

The wishes of the survivors are followed. The organs will not be donated, even if the donor has signed a donor card, if the survivors do not concur. The importance of discussing a decision to donate should always be communicated with family and friends.

♡ Who Will Remove The Organs?

Organ procurement agencies have donor surgeons on call at all times, who are trained for the procedure. The surgery will be performed in the hospital where the donor has died.

Donor surgeons from other organ procurement programs may participate in the surgical procedure if organs will be used in other hospitals. Organs are often transported to distant hospitals and transplanted into waiting patients. Due to tight constrictions because of preservation times, time is of the essence. Life support equipment is used before surgery to maintain the necessary blood supply to the organs.

♡ Costs

All costs related to organ procurement are covered by a government program and/or insurance that benefits patients receiving transplants.

♡ Funeral Arrangements

Removal of organs will not interfere with customary funeral arrangements. The funeral director is notified upon completion of the surgery. Regular funeral costs, memorial services or burial plans remain the responsibility of the family or estate.

♡ Confidentiality

The identity of patients who receive the transplanted organs, and the donors remain confidential. Generally, the Transplant Coordinators are available to answer most questions regarding the donation.

Shortly after my transplant, I wrote a letter to the donor's family, thanking them and their loved one for the gift of life. The letter was given to the organ procurement agency for delivery to the family. My name and all identification was removed from the letter to insure confidentiality.

The procurement agency will decide whether the patient's family would benefit from receiving the letter. If some benefit will be derived, the letter will be delivered. If benefit will not be gained by the family, the letter will be maintained by the agency. I have informed the agency that if the family would care to know anything regarding the recipient, that all questions should be answered. I want the family to know, that their act of love has meant an extended, full life to me.

♡ How to become a donor

Express an interest, and communicate your desire with a relative. Although you may want to be a donor, the hospital or procurement agency will always ask the spouse, parent or next of kin if they wish for your organs to be donated. If they are not asked, or if they express any negative feeling, the organs will not be donated. Make sure your desires are presented in a positive manner to your family.

Under a Federal law enacted in the mid- eighties, hospitals are required to ask about organ donation. However, many times the procedure is not followed, as in the case of Dusty Futrall.

Often, the decision is left with the survivors, who do not know, or cannot understand the position of the deceased. In many cases, the delay in making a decision renders the organs and tissues unsuitable for transplant. In my case, one of the hearts suitable for transplant was wasted because of the long delay in making a decision. The measures taken to preserve the heart eventually caused a deterioration of its condition.

Sign your driver's license or organ donor card, and be sure to communicate your desires with your loved ones.

♡ Alleviating the Shortage

The critical shortage of available organs can only be eased by a number of alternatives and actions:

1. Development of self powered mechanical organs, including the heart.
2. Increased donor awareness campaigns to stimulate organ donors.
3. Development of improved preservation techniques to increase ischemic time.
4. Development of techniques to transfer animal organs to humans.
5. Payment of fees to donors, or survivors.

♡ Development of Self Powered Mechanical Devices

Development work has been extensive, in attempts to develop portable, self contained powered portable devices. The available options are powered by equipment residing external to the body.

The external power sources for most heart assist devices are connected to the heart by tubes leading through the chest cavity. The power source is bulky, weighing several hundred pounds, and severely limits mobility to within several yards of the device. In addition, access to the body lends itself to infection. Because of the immobility, the quality of life is poor, at best.

The most well known recipient of a mechanical heart was Barney Clark, a retired dentist, who gained renown in 1982. He lived 112 days before succumbing to heart failure.

Most mechanical hearts carry a high risk of infection due to the body orifice required, and a high incidence of strokes.

The problem will be reduced when an implantable power packs or batteries can be implanted under the skin to power the mechanical heart. Development of a power source alleviate a major problem, and afford the recipient a higher quality of life.

♡ Increase Donor Awareness

The primary method of becoming an organ donor is to sign a driver's license or organ donor card.

Organ transplantation has been shown to be favored by the vast majority of American citizens, with most polls indicating an approval rate exceeding 80% of the population. Actual organ donations, however, occur in only 2% of the deaths in this country.

The reasons for the low occurrence include taboos regarding religious beliefs, fear that all steps will not be taken by health care professionals to save the life of a potential donor, potential donors with previous health or drug problems, age of the potential donor, and method of death. At least 25,000 people die each year whose organs could be used to enhance the lives of people waiting for organs.

Approximately 1/3 of all people on waiting lists for hearts or livers will die waiting, due to the lack of available organs. In addition, many others could have an improved quality of life if kidneys, pancreases, corneas or other tissues were available for transplant.

I have written countless letters to political personnel, attempting to encourage organ donations. Several proposals included the enclosure of facsimile donor cards in the newsletters of Congressmen, as well as magazines. In addition, one proposal would give the opportunity for students at state supported universities to check off whether they desired to be organ donors. The current method of soliciting donors when drivers renew their licenses is inadequate, since the registrar may forget to ask the prospective donor, and the question is only asked once every several years.

In the United States, we have a voluntary system of organ donation called required consent, while in many European countries, the organ becomes the property of the country (presumed consent).

In one case, the donor has to sign a pledge to donate the organ. In the other instance, the donor has to sign a statement forbidding the state from using the organs. Although some have argued for presumed consent in our country, the spirit of volunteerism would be broached, and the movement would not have favor.

I believe we can increase the number of donors by increasing public awareness of the issue, and for recipients to become active advocates of transplantation. Studies have also reported that only a small percentage of potential donors had heard, or known, someone who had benefitted from an organ donation. Our citizens will help each other if they are informed of the shortage, and the miracle of the "Gift of Life".

The media in Zanesville was very supportive in publicizing transplants in our community, and there was renewed interest. On several occasions, people stopped me in the street or grocery store to discuss transplants, and to show their organ donor cards. Much of the mystery of transplants can be removed if potential donors see the benefit of transplants. Those who have had transplants must make efforts to speak to more civic, professional, church or school groups.

Our governments must also make it easier to become donors. My brother Joe attempted to become a donor in Maryland, and was told he would have to send to the Department of Motor Vehicles for a form, to be signed and notarized before being returned for approval. Although the law was subsequently changed to facilitate organ donation, the process, country wide should be easier.

I was once disappointed in the Ohio method when I renewed my license after the transplant. The sticker on the back of the license had been removed due to an effort to implement a national driver's license, and replaced by a sticker on the front of the license and a separate donor card. Worse yet, only a few people knew of the change, and efforts to solicit donors fell upon the clerks in the registrars's offices, who frequently did not ask if applicants wanted to be donors. I wrote a letter to the local media, as well as the state, and the explanations indicated a complete lack of understanding of the cost or effectiveness of the revised method.

The inconsistency of obtaining donors was reflected in enormous disparities of organ donors between districts or counties, and measured the effectiveness of the registrars.

♡ Improved Preservation Techniques

A critical factor limiting the number of transplants is the ischemic, or preservation times. The ischemic time is the length of time between the harvest of an organ from a donor, and the installation into a recipient. The time varies between organs, with the heart's ischemic time approximately four hours before deterioration begins to occur.

If the ischemic time could be increased through the development of improved preservation techniques, the additional organs could be saved for transplant. In today's environment, some organs are procured in far away states, and flown to hospitals by teams of procurement specialists.

Many of the successful transplant programs in the United States use private jets to rush organs from procurement locations to hospitals where transplants are preformed. One of the potential hearts for my transplant was in New Jersey, that would have been on the envelope of distance.

The area served is partially a function of the ischemic time, since an organ must be implanted into a recipient within a strict time span. Current records include hearts at 8 hours, livers at 6 hours and kidneys at 72 hours. An experimental 10 ingredient solution developed at the University of Wisconsin in 1987 preserved animal livers for 24 hours.

Advances in technology could increase the available supply for transplant. A new preservative developed by Dupont, called ViaSpan, has in many cases tripled preservation time.

♡ Use of Animal Organs

The use of animal organs for transplants into humans have been rare. I recall an attempt during the latter part of 1984 to transplant the heart of a baboon into an infant "Baby Fae" in California. The little girl lived

21 days with the monkey heart. There was an uproar by animal rights groups protesting the action. It should be noted that parts of animals are sometimes used in transplants. Heart valves from pigs are sometimes used in humans.

The hearts of pigs closely represent those of humans. There have been various proposals to genetically engineer pigs, and use the hearts for transplantation into humans. Although the proposal would cause an uproar with animal rights groups, we should remember that animals are currently being raised, and slaughtered, for less urgent reasons that saving lives.

Researchers at the University of Minnesota are attempting to develop a new species of pigs with genetically engineered human proteins to fight organ rejection. The first group of pigs will be born in 1992, with transplants possible by the end of the decade.

The biggest problem is currently rejection. The human genes will create proteins similar to those that identify blood types. It is hoped that the rejection by the body's immune system will decrease. Currently, most attempts to transfer animal hearts to humans have experienced in immediate and violent rejection.

The advantages of using pigs are that 1/2 of all children born with congenital heart disease may be helped with a transplant from a pig, and pigs can be grown in various sizes. They are also not an endangered species.

♡ Payment For Organs

There have been endless debates regarding payment for transplantable organs. I had watched an interesting television program several years ago, concerning convicts about to be executed. The convicts had proposed selling their organs, with their families receiving the funds.

Their argument was that the transplant industry had winners and losers, with the winners receiving cash payment or benefit. The doctors, nurses, hospitals, drug companies, procurement agencies and recipients received money or an improved life. The donors or their families received nothing except the knowledge that the organs had extended the life of a stranger.

When the audience became hostile toward the rationale, the convicts asked how many hospitals or doctors performed the operations for free. The convicts stated if humanitarian reasons were the only reasons for transplants, many hospitals would perform the operations at no cost to the patient. He added that transplants were a business, and would be stopped if a profit could not be made by the procedures, or the research programs at the institutions.

The arguments are endless, and also lead to conclusions that poor people in the country would be taken advantage of by rich people requiring transplants. The United Network of Organ Sharing (UNOS) was established in 1986 to prevent the buying and selling of organs, and act as a clearinghouse for the fair distribution of available organs, based upon need.

A law passed in 1984 made it illegal in the United States to buy and sell organs. Violators can be fined $ 50,000 or face up to 5 years in prison. UNOS was established to eliminate widespread abuses in organ distribution. At one time, monetary considerations, including the payment of "bounties" almost caused the end of transplant programs in this country.

Advocates of buying organs argue that the shortage of many organs would be solved if sufficient monetary incentive was offered to survivors. The free market would insure an adequate supply if funeral costs or a death benefit was paid.

I had several different views of incentive payments during my illness, and wait in the various hospitals. When your condition is critical, and every day is borrowed, there is nothing more important than having a chance to live. I was originally in favor of voluntary donations, but as the days and weeks turned into months, I began to favor either presumed consent, as practiced in many European countries, or payment to donors to increase the supply.

As with any proposal, I do not know whether the payment of a few thousand dollars would increase the supply. Personally, I do not think the monetary incentive will work. Either a person is committed to help someone else, or the money will not make any difference. The payment could open up serious abuses that occurred prior to the formation of UNOS, and who would say the payments could escalate to levels where only rich people would have transplants. The payments could also be in direct proportion to the sickness of the patient. Would a man sacrifice everything that their family owned at a chance to stay alive for a few months?

I continue to favor increased donor awareness. Our country is great because people will help each other if they know there is a problem, without the payment of funds for transplantable organs.

♡ Josh Joseph

David's friend Josh Joseph kids me about being a transplant patient, and makes fun of my high-top Reebook athletic shoes that I purchased for the daily walks. I tell him that he isn't sophisticated enough to wear shoes like mine.

♡ Church Support

I received hundreds of cards and letters offering encouragement, and each day brought an outpouring of love and concern from various church members, including many from Sunday School students.

A friend from McGraw-Edison, Greg Quinton, was an active member of the Zane Trace Church of Christ, a small congregation in Zanesville. Each week brought many cards and words of encouragement. After the operation, we attended one of their services at Zane Trace. I suspect that on a per member basis, I received more support from the tiny church than any other church.

Groups from my home church sent many, many cards including messages from the Sunday School children, the ladies's circles and the Quilters, a group of ladies that meet to quilt, and donate the proceeds to worthy projects. Several members of the church, Bob England and Treasure Ulster even made home made soup and chili. Bette Kullman, one of my favorite ladies, made cake and desserts. Vangie Cunningham, Gloria Crooks, Gene Wolfe, Delores Soufis and Ellen Shaw sent cards and letters at least weekly. The support and encouragement from the congregation was endless.

Other churches in Zanesville included our family in prayer chains, praying for a miracle.

Another church with many caring individuals was our old church, the Lutheran Church of St. Andrew in Franklin, Tennessee. During my stay in Vanderbilt, I had many visits from Cheryl Bucher and her in-laws, Bill and Jennet, as well as Wanda McIntyre and Harold and Doris Catron. We had met them when we attended St. Andrew in the late 1970's. Jennet would bring home made cookies, many of which were eaten by my cardiologist, Ted Eastburn.

The Pastor of Trinity Evangelical Lutheran Church in Zanesville, Ohio, Reverend Larry Kudart, and the congregation have taken active roles in promoting organ donation.

Zanesville was characterized as a dying town with slumping downtown church attendance in a recent study. Evidently the individual who was quick to make a hasty judgement, never met Reverend Kudart, or attended a service at Trinity. What an uplifting experience! The walls and atmosphere are full of excitement as we hear of God's miracles. The building is always packed for both services.

I am always quick to point out that the Bible mentions the healing power of Jesus, and we've all heard of how he cured several believers of various maladies. If we compare the Biblical text with actual experience, we can see that transplants enable current miracles to occur. Transplants enable sick people to have fuller and longer lives, and for blind people to see. Transplants are a miracle, limited only to the supply of organs available for transplant.

Pastor Kudart requested that I address the adult Sunday School class at Trinity. In addition, the Vicar, Wayne Palmer, brought the high school confirmation class. It was a great experience to tell others about the "Gift of Life" and how my life had been positively affected by a transplant. I believe that the more publicity brought to the attention of the general public, the greater the acceptance of transplants.

♡ Artificial Hearts

Artificial hearts are not currently a viable solution to the shortage, due to the lack of an implantable power source.

The first patent for an artificial heart was developed by Paul Winchell, the famous ventriloquist of Jerry Mahoney fame! The patent was filed in

1963, when Winchell, dabbling as an inventor, was studying medicine at Columbia University under the developer of the Heimlich maneuver.

The patent was donated to the University of Utah, which later hired a young doctor named Robert Jarvick. Jarvick refined Winchell's invention, and received credit for developing the Jarvick 7 heart.

When Jarvick was 36, the mechanical heart was implanted in a retired dentist, Barney Clark, on December 2, 1982 during a 7 1/2 hour surgery. Clark received a great deal of notoriety prior to his death 112 days later from other organ complications.

Production of the Jarvick 7 was stopped in December 1990 due to manufacturing irregularities. It is used only as a bridge in critical situations. The major drawbacks include the external power source, which severely limits mobility, the tendency for increased clotting and possibility of increased strokes or infection.

♡ AIDS

The transplantation of organs involves a degree of risk concerning AIDS.

In May, 1991, the country was informed of a number of patients who had died when organs from a murder victim where transplanted into several patients. In addition, a large number of tissues from the donor had also been transplanted. A nationwide search took place, attempting to locate the recipients of the man's tissues. The media delved into the young man's background.

Although the young man had the AIDS virus, multiple tests did not reflect the infection. It was surmised he had contracted the disease immediately prior to the testing, when the presence of the malady would not appear. Tests were also done in many of the hospitals where the organs and tissues were transplanted.

Subsequent extensive questioning of the young man's friends and acquaintances revealed his habits to be non compatible with many AIDS victims...he was heterosexual and not an IV drug user. At the same time, the American Red Cross announced a nationwide revamping of blood testing procedures, including the consolidation of certain laboratories, retraining of personnel and much tighter quality control procedures.

An addition theory surfaced...the young man had been given

transfusions prior to the recovery of the organs. It appears possible that one of the transfusions contained tainted blood.

I thought many times about the AIDS virus when I was waiting for a heart. One of the potential donors was suspected to be an IV drug user. Apparently, the individual had lost a significant amount of weight prior to being shot. The donor was checked, and caution was exercised in not accepting the heart for transplant.

I read several articles regarding the young man in Virginia suspected of having AIDS. One of the articles concerned the effect of the publicity on his mother, who had been harassed by the media, and others, concerning her son. She had been openly criticized for allowing her son's organs to be transplanted. I wrote to the mother, assuring her that she had made the right decision in attempting to give others an opportunity to benefit from her son's death. I labeled her a hero for her generosity, and remarked that many people could attain an improved quality of life if more people would become organ donors.

Several friends asked if I were worried about contracting AIDS. I remarked that I had lived 18 months longer than I deserved, and I was grateful for the extra time that I had spent with my family. I felt anyone in the same position as I, would have risked almost anything to have an opportunity to live a little longer.

There was speculation that the number of people on waiting lists would decrease due to the fear of contracting AIDS. This will not happen. The probability of contracting an infectious disease is infinitesimal, and is safer with each day. I hope the publicity will encourage more people to become potential donors. Many lives can be saved if more organs and tissues become available.

♡ Informing the public

In an attempt to increase the donor pool in Ohio, I enlisted the aid of several elected officials. My plan was to introduce legislation that would enable college students to be given an opportunity to sign donor cards whenever they registered each quarter at state supported institutions. I felt the current method of enlistment, the request at the time of license renewal, was erratic and insufficient.

My state representative, Paul Mechling, called several months after I had sent the original letter. Paul had scheduled a meeting with the Deans of the state supported medical schools. He mentioned the approach was to sell the concept to the deans first, and the Presidents of the universities would follow.

Barb and I traveled to Columbus during the first week of June, a beautiful morning in Ohio's largest city. We met Paul in the lobby of the state office tower, and caught an elevator to the 37th floor. Barb and I were very impressed with the building...it was very similar to the Cooper Industries headquarters building in Houston, where I had attended several meetings.

We were escorted into a room with a large conference table. Seated around the table were representatives of the state supported medical schools. After a few minutes, I was introduced, and told the story of the critical shortage of donors, not only in Ohio but nationwide. The attendees asked several questions regarding the reason why only 2% of deaths resulted in organ donations. I responded that the taboos involved, the difficulty of asking for or receiving consent made it very difficult for health care professionals or donor families in our country. I felt the decision to become a donor is best made when the donor is in a position to evaluate their position, and to inform the immediate family.

♡ Epilogue

John died on March 9, 1997, at Mercy Hospital in Pittsburgh, PA. He was 54 years old. He died exactly 30 years from the day of our first date, March 9, 1967.

He had lived seven years and five months with his new heart. He always said that any time he lived after the day of his transplant, October 9, 1989, was just "gravy on the mashed potatoes of life". He lived and loved every extra day he was given. He not only saw his first grandson, Sebastian, born, but he saw his first granddaughter, Asia, born also. He got to see both of his children graduate, and he got to walk his daughter down the aisle.

He spent the extra seven years promoting transplantation. He and Simon Keith got together and organized soccer clinics throughout the country, encouraging young people to enjoy the sport of soccer and teaching them about taking care of their bodies and the miracle of transplantation. He spoke about transplantation to schools, churches, and other organizations. He especially enjoyed speaking to the young people.

His funeral was held at St. John Lutheran Church in Zanesville, Ohio, and was a celebration of his life. Andy Mast, the little boy he took to McDonald's after receiving his new heart, carried the cross at the funeral. Pastor Alden Towberman officiated at the funeral. His friend, Pastor Jim Couts, spoke words of remembrance. His friend, Ellen Shaw, was the organist. John's friend, Anne England, sang his favorite hymn, and her husband, Dr. Bob England, along with Mike Tandy, Bruce Evans, Joseph Kennedy, Darrel Clifford, and Jack Downing were pallbearers.

In loving memory,
Barbara

John's friend, Bill Tschudy, read the following message that John had written before his death and requested to be read at his funeral.

"Dear friends and family,
   Thanks for coming today.
   I believe your presence will bring great comfort to my family.
   Today should be a day of celebration.
   I have been so fortunate in life to have had you as my friends and relatives. What greater joy can someone have in life than to experience a full life with friends and family.
   My family has brought me great joy, from my wonderful and caring wife, Barbara, to our children, David and Beth, and my grandson, Sebastian, and my wonderful granddaughter, Asia.
   I had hoped to accomplish more in life to help others. I will leave that task to each of you to help others and continue to do things each day that will help others.
   I only ask that you never give up in trying to make it a better community and a better world.

John"

♡ About the Author

John M. Garrett was forty-five years old when he received his heart transplant, and with his final years in life he dedicated himself to promoting organ donation and transplantation. As a legacy to help make a better world, Wait until Tuesday has been posthumously published by his loving and caring wife, Barbara.

Printed in the United States
By Bookmasters